Irina Rodnina and Alexander Zaitsev were never beaten in competition because of their daring and sureness in difficult lifts like this

Jayne Torvill and Christopher Dean demonstrate the immaculate style which took them to the top

The BBC Book of Skating

Sandra Stevenson

British Broadcasting Corporation

Sandra Stevenson has attended every skating World Championship and Winter Olympic Games since 1968. A former skater, she has passed five National Skating Association's tests, and has appeared in several professional ice shows. She has been the ice skating correspondent for the Guardian *since 1971, and is the leading writer for* Ice and Roller Skate *magazine.*

Picture credits

ALL SPORT **frontcover**, **back cover** *left*, **1, 5** (Adrian Murrell) 6 *top*, **8** *bottom*, **12** *bottom*, **13** (Tony Duffy), 19 *left*, 24 *bottom*, **29** *top left* and *bottom*, **32** (all Tony Duffy), 58 *right* (Tony Duffy), 63 *right*, 74 *bottom left* (Tony Duffy), 77 *right* (Tony Duffy), 81 *left* (Tony Duffy), 83 *right* (Tony Duffy), 87 *left*, 91 (Syndication International), **104** *top* (Tony Duffy), **108** *top* and *bottom* (both Tony Duffy), 110, **113** *top*, 115 *left* (Steve Powell), **117**, **120** *bottom left* (Steve Powell) and *right* (Tony Duffy), **124, 125** (3 photos Adrian Murrell), 128; MRS. BARRY 59 *right*; BBC HULTON PICTURE LIBRARY 39, 41 *left* and *right*, 50 *left* and 51 *left* (both Evening Standard Collection); JEAN BURNIER 11 *left*; INGRID BUTT 33, 47, 65 *left*, 77 *left*, 87 *right*, 98 *right*, **101** *top*, **105, 109** *top*, **116** (3 photos), **120** *top*, 143 *top left*, 148 *top*; HOWEY CAUFMAN **29** *top right*, 58 *left*, 72 *right*, 98 *left*, **100, 101** *bottom left*, **109** *bottom*, **112**, 126 *left*, 129, 135 *top right*, 136 *top*, 139 *left*, 141 *bottom left*, 143 *bottom right*; MIKE COSGROVE **back cover** *right*, **21**, **97** *top* and *bottom*, **113** *bottom*, **121**, 131 *left* and *right*, 132, 135 *top left* and *bottom right*, 136 *bottom left*, 148 *bottom right*; DAILY MAIL 56; INTERNATIONAL NEWS PHOTO 44; M. KNEPPER 61; KOBAL COLLECTION 28 *bottom*; NOVOSTI PRESS AGENCY 94 *left*, 140 *bottom right*; POPPERFOTO 45 *left* and *right*, 49 *left*, 81 *right*, 140 *top left* and *right* (UPI), 141 *top left* (AFP); PRESS ASSOCIATION 49 *right*; CELIA ROBERTS 50 *right*; SKATE MAGAZINE (Fred Dean) **8** *top*, **9**, 11 *right*, **12** *top*, 14 *left* and *right*, **16, 17**, 19 *right*, **20**, 24 *top*, **25**, 27 *left* and *right*, 35 *left* and *right*, 65 *right*, 70 *left* and *right*, 72 *left*, 74 *right*, 83 *left*, 89 *left* and *right*, 94 *right*, 96 *left* and *right*, **101** *bottom right*, 103 *right*, **104** *bottom*, 115 *right*, 118, 135 *bottom left*, 136 *bottom right* (Winfried Terres), 139 *right*, 140 *bottom left*, 141 *top right*, 143 *top right* and *bottom left*, 144 (4 photos), 146, 147 *top left* and *right*, 148 *bottom left*, 149 (3 photos); SPORT & GENERAL PRESS 46; SPORTING PICTURES (UK) 2; CHERYL SWISHER **4**, 53, 63 *left*, 74 *centre left*, 147 *bottom*; **32** *top*; UNITED FEATURE SYNDICATE INC © 1971 133; UPI 6 *bottom* (Matti Bjorkman – Lehtikuva Oy), 37 (Matti Bjorkman – Lehtikuva Oy), 74 *top left* (Ari Ojala – Lehtikuva Oy), 103 *left* (AFP), 126 *right* (Hartmut Reeh – DPA); R. WAGSTAFF 59 *left*; JOHN WILSON MARSDEN BROS & CO **28** *top*.

Published by the
British Broadcasting Corporation
35 Marylebone High Street
London W1M 4AA

ISBN 0 563 20223 8

First published 1984
© Sandra Stevenson 1984

Printed in England by
Jolly & Barber Ltd, Rugby

Contents

Karen Barber and Nicky Slater's new Charlie Chaplin routine

Jayne and Chris's 1983 'Barnum on Ice' made history . . .

. . . gaining an unprecedented perfect flush of sixes

1

Torvill and Dean
Simply the Best

In 1982 and 1983, by awarding higher marks than ever before, the International Skating Union (ISU) judges acclaimed Britain's Jayne Torvill and Christopher Dean the best ice dancers the world has known. Through their competitive performances, televised in almost every country in the world, they have gained more publicity for their home town, Nottingham, than anyone since Errol Flynn played Robin Hood.

Yet had they been born in any other city they probably would not have started skating. Unlike John Curry, who was inspired to take up the sport after seeing an ice show on television, outside influences brought Torvill and Dean to the ageing Nottingham Ice Stadium in Lower Parliament Street near the city centre. Jayne's school had a programme in which pupils were taken to the rink. She was nearly ten and hated putting on the ugly, black, worn rental skates. She pestered her parents, who run a small newsagent's shop, to buy her a pair of second-hand skates. With this precious acquisition and a private lesson a week, Jayne was hooked.

Chris's stepmother pointed him on the path which was to bring him world-wide fame. She bought him a pair of new skates and took him to the rink hoping that this would provide the ten-year-old with an interest to keep him off the streets and out of mischief after school. At first Mrs Dean would stay with him at the rink. The first time she left him on his own she returned to be greeted by the news that he was at hospital. He had skated into the rink barrier and broken a leg. 'I just forgot to stop,' Chris said when asked how the accident had occurred.

For most children that accident would have meant the swift end of their skating career. Betty Dean certainly would have preferred him to take up something less risky. However, by this time Chris was committed. Almost immediately the cast came off he passed his preliminary test, though one of the three judges pointed out he appeared a little stiff on one side. Chris was so promising that when his father, an electrician, was laid off work due to a strike, his first instructress, Pat Beet, approached his parents offering to accept delayed payment so that Chris would not have to miss any lessons.

Betty Callaway keeps her eyes on both sets of pupils – Kristina Regoeczy and Andras Sallay are on the ice, and Jayne and Chris wait their turn (at an international at Richmond in 1979)

A dream come true: winning their first international championship in 1981 (beating the Olympic gold medallists, Natalia Linichuk and Gennadi Karponosov, in blue, and former World champions, Irina Moiseeva and Andrei Minenkov)

Intricate footwork from Jayne and Chris's 'Mack and Mabel' routine

Initially Jayne and Chris were teamed with different partners and both couples were very successful. Jayne, knowing that she had taken up the sport a little late to do well as a singles skater, was fearless and determined in lifts with a very fallible partner, Michael Hutchinson. They won the British junior pair title and represented Britain in the St Gervais Grand Prix in France and the Nebelhorn Trophy in Oberstdorf in southern Germany. Then, when she was fourteen, they won the British senior pair title. However, a few weeks later, having been placed last in the European Pair Championship in Göteborg, the partnership split.

Nottingham is the centre of British ice dancing. The national championships have been held there since 1951. It is impossible for anyone to skate at this rink without being influenced by ice dancing and this was the direction Chris chose. He teamed with the tall Sandra Elson.

Sandra and Chris won the 1972 British novice championship, a remarkable achievement since they managed to fall in two of the three compulsory dances. At this stage Sandra was distinctly the better technician. A photograph taken the following year shows a rather podgy Chris in a very bad position on the back edge after the Foxtrot outside mohawk. However, Sandra's excellent presence on the ice enabled them to gain fifth place in the British junior championship only slightly behind Nicky Slater and his first partner, Kathryn Winter. Nicky would never have believed that Chris, carried as he then was by Sandra's abilities, would later overtake him and that he himself would become a perennial second-place competitor. In 1974 they won the British junior title and were selected for their first international, in Czechoslovakia. They nearly didn't take part: there was a problem in obtaining Chris's visa, possibly because he had become a police cadet.

The junior ice dance title is said to be unlucky. With only one exception none of the winners has gone on to win the senior championship. Either their partnership has dissolved or the couple has been eclipsed by those they had beaten. In Sandra and Chris's case they started quarrelling. Their coach, Len Sayward, left Nottingham to become the manager of Grimsby ice rink and Sandra and Chris started training with Janet Sawbridge who had just taken up a teaching post at the Nottingham rink after being presented with an MBE for her services to the sport. With three different partners Janet had represented Britain in the international championships for over a decade, and had never been placed lower than seventh. Within a week she was in despair over Chris and Sandra's obvious incompatibility. Sandra decided it was just too much. Their partnership terminated, some said because of the jinx on the junior title.

When the news became public that Chris was looking for a partner several possible candidates made it known that they were available. Janet suggested that Chris give Jayne, who had taken ice dance lessons from

Jayne, and her first partner, Michael
Hutchinson, compete in a French international

Chris and Sandra Elson take part in the 1973
British junior championship

Len, a try-out. Jayne had seen the handsome Chris around the rink and
had heard about his offhand treatment of Sandra. She was interested but
extremely nervous. Their try-out was arranged for early morning and
Jayne says she remembers little about it except that she could hardly
keep her eyes open.

Rumour had it that Chris was going to be matched with a stunning-
looking girl from another rink. Few gave Jayne much chance. They
didn't appear to be well matched physically, and Jayne was not of the
same standard as Chris. However, Janet saw some quality in Chris and
Jayne's performance together that was lost to others, and she appreciated
Jayne's speed and basic skating ability, developed while she was in pairs
competition.

The newly formed couple showed so much promise in practice that
the National Skating Association (NSA) took the unprecedented step of
entering them in the 1976 summer contests in St Gervais and Oberstdorf
before they had competed together in England. They did not let the
selectors down, coming second in Germany to a Russian couple who
were to finish fifth in the following World Championship, and winning
the French event, although Jayne had been sick all the previous week and
Chris collapsed as they got to the end of their routine. He was treated in

In their 'Mack and Mabel' routine Jayne and Chris, for the first time, attempted to tell a story

Jayne, Chris and Betty Callaway at the picturesquely situated West German Training Centre

'Barnum' was meant to convey the atmosphere of the circus. Here the high-wire artists intertwine their legs in improbable, difficult and highly dangerous positions

Left Jayne and Chris's partnership looked promising right from the start . . .

Above . . . winning their first British title, November 1978 (second were Karen Barber and Nicky Slater, who have yet to escape their shadow; third were Kathryn Winter and Kim Spreyer)

hospital with a saline drip to counter dehydration caused by a gastric flu virus, and released after two days, missing the celebration of their and Robin Cousins's victories.

Jayne and Chris's routine was well received by the judges but criticised in other quarters. Jayne had brought over some novel moves from her pair-skating days, and they did a version of a death spiral and of a cartwheel that many thought were not in keeping with traditional ice dancing. Their innovations still meet with some criticism. Even their splendid 'Barnum' free dance, which gained for them a third World title in 1983, has been decried as mere pantomime, in spite of the judges' unhesitating approval.

In St Gervais Chris had just turned eighteen and Jayne was a few months older. Their performance served notice to the skating world that a new power was about to emerge. That November, in the British senior championship, they gained third place in the original set pattern (OSP) division but were pipped for the bronze overall by a 4–5 decision. It was an impressive debut in the national competition and observers were particularly struck by the speed with which they tossed off their foot-work. The next summer they gained another international win, this time in Oberstdorf, demonstrating an extremely flamboyant Paso Doble OSP. (This rhythm was chosen for the 1984 Olympic season's OSP.) In 1977 Chris showed his understanding of the intent of this dance, swirling Jayne around him as if she were his cape and had no will of her own.

In the 1977 British senior championship they gained third place and selection for the European and World Championship teams for Strasbourg and Ottawa. Janet Sawbridge, in an advanced stage of pregnancy, accompanied them to France, to see them placed a creditable ninth, but could not be with them in Canada. There, in a lift, they spoke their first words to Betty Callaway who was to become a major factor in their path to the top. She trains only one, or at the most two, couples at a time, and was teaching Kristina Regoeczy and Andras Sallay of Hungary who were then thinking of retiring. Fortunately they changed their minds and went on to become the 1980 World champions, the first non-Russians to hold this title since 1969. By then Betty Callaway had committed herself to training Jayne and Chris, and so the Hungarians moved into a flat in Nottingham and spent most of the year there.

Betty is the sort of cultured, soft-spoken, middle-aged woman with an iron will who, in another century, would have taken her Union Jack and set out to civilise the world. She started skating when the convent school she attended decided this was acceptable physical activity for Wednesday afternoons. She then shocked her parents by deciding she no longer wished to attend school and was off to join an ice show. She married her partner in that ice show and eventually started teaching at the Richmond ice rink. Her former husband, Roy Callaway, recalls that she was extremely shy in those days and he suggested she took ice dance lessons from Gladys Hogg to upgrade her own qualifications. Amongst the many skaters she taught at the Richmond rink were Princess Anne and other members of the royal family. However, her first pupils to have a major international success were Angelika Buck and her brother Erich, the 1972 European champions, whom Betty taught while she was the West German national coach.

Very few people have heard Betty raise her voice. In all the years in which they were trained by her, the Hungarians remember that this happened only once. Andy said he and Kristina were going at each other hammer and tongs and Mrs Callaway, standing at the rink barrier, told them to be quiet in no uncertain manner. They were so shocked they completely forgot what they had been fighting about.

Jayne and Chris say that they owe Kristina and Andy a great deal. The friendly rivalry between the two couples eased the daily slog, and since the Hungarians were at a higher level, there was a lot to be learnt from them. They had won bronze medals in the World Championship in Ottawa while Chris and Jayne were eleventh. In November 1978 Chris and Jayne won the first of a series of British titles. Though the British

'Barnum' again – Chris prepares to swing Jayne between his legs so that her head will barely clear the ice in a trick guaranteed to win great applause

The quickness of Jayne and Chris's criss-crossing legs in these fast-paced sequences
astonished knowledgeable spectators

senior championship had been held in Nottingham for the previous twenty eight years, this was the first time a local couple had won. With their win came an extra prize – their first 'six', the maximum mark given in skating, awarded to them by Mollie Phillips, the judge who had also given John Curry his first six. November 1983 should bring them their sixth British senior title; no other couple has won more than four, although Courtney Jones won five times with two partners.

Before their second European Championship, in Zagreb in 1979, Chris and Jayne went with Betty and the Hungarian champions to train in Budapest, where they had private ice at reasonable times of the day. (In Nottingham they had had to train after midnight.) They were also able to work with advanced video equipment. The progress they had made showed clearly, for they advanced three places. It might have been more had not Chris almost fallen in the first compulsory when his skate caught in a rut. A more experienced couple would have anticipated the problem and moved the projected pattern of the dance slightly to avoid the bad ice. They learnt the hard way that in addition to ability, a successful pair needs to possess competition 'smarts'.

A few weeks later in the World Championship in Vienna, while the Hungarians were taking the silver medals and gaining their first international six, Jayne and Chris were down in eighth place – not spectacular, but definitely on the upward curve. They impressed the ISU officials so much with their ability in the compulsory dance portion that they were chosen over higher-ranked competitors to demonstrate 'the Blues' compulsory dance in the ISU's instructional film. Shortly afterwards, they gained silver medals in a contest at Morzine, France. Later that year they were silver medallists twice again, coming behind the Hungarians in the Rotary Watches contest in Britain, and in the NHK Trophy in Tokyo being only narrowly beaten by the Russians, Irina Moiseeva and Andrei Minenkov. They returned from Japan in an extremely elated mood. To think they had almost been placed ahead of the legendary Min and Mo, the 1975 and 1977 World champions who were competing in the World Championships more than two years before Jayne and Chris teamed up. They had often watched Mo's famous tragedian act, enhanced by her sleepy, sensuous, half-closed eyes, on television.

Betty was driving them hard and improvement was coming. They had gained some television exposure from the Rotary Watches contest, but many people first became aware of them when the BBC came to Nottingham in November 1979, the first time it had covered the British ice dance championship since the late 1960s. The BBC was sufficiently pleased with the outcome to televise the event twice, the day afterwards and the following Wednesday on *Sportsnight*. The general public, seeing these programmes, began to appreciate the tall, blond policeman and his tiny, unassuming partner.

However, the hard work was beginning to cause a strain. They were constantly tired. Jayne was working as an insurance clerk. Chris was coming to dread making arrests, with all the attendant paperwork and court appearances which would eat into his free time. Often they felt like zombies as they ripped around the Nottingham rink well after midnight. They both shuddered when discussing how much time off work was required to fit in skating competitions. Though their employers were sympathetic, even more practice time would be needed for the Olympic season.

Unlike most newcomers, they didn't make the mistake of trying to copy the established stars. They worked at developing their own style. In 1980, in Göteborg, they came fourth in the European event. John Curry has said that fourth is the worst place to finish. You know you have done well, yet you have not won a place on the rostrum. However Jayne and Chris felt hopeful. The Olympics were taking place in a few weeks and there was at least a possibility that they might win a medal. British media interest was focused on Robin Cousins and so very little pressure was put on them.

Yet, at Lake Placid they felt unexpectedly down. Their accommodation did not help. It was literally comprised of cells. After the Olympics this newly built facility was converted into a federal prison which houses fewer prisoners than it did athletes. The bus schedule to the ice rink was somewhat erratic and the competition spread over a greater timespan

Once they decided to skate full time their progress was obvious and rapid

Note the steep angle their left blades make with the ice and their perfect unison

Chris and Jayne's white 'Barnum' outfits raised quite a few eyebrows, though they strikingly conveyed the world of the circus

The climax comes as Chris flips Jayne over his head. Many people maintained this pantomine element had no place in amateur ice dancing, but the judges did not concur

than at a World Championship, feeding already edgy nerves. Since the amount of practice time allotted them was infinitely less than their daily training programme at home, most competitors found their standard dropping. Jayne and Chris, suffering from an unusual languor, couldn't muster their normal zest, and to cap matters Jayne came down with the Olympic flu. They finished fifth. However, they ended their Lake Placid stay on a high note, for when Regoeczy and Sallay, silver medallists to Linichuk and Karponosov, were also hit by Olympic flu they accepted the invitation to replace them in the exhibition programme.

A few weeks later, at the World Championships in Dortmund, they performed the compulsory dances so well they were in contention at that stage for the bronze medals. It was particularly disappointing, then, when Jayne made a mistake in the OSP. She tensed up, the worst thing that can happen, and then did so again in the next sequence. She rushed off the ice and collapsed in tears in the dressing room. Chris, used to Jayne never making a mistake, could hardly take in what had happened. It was a very unhappy moment, and they finished fourth.

Their greatest ambition now was to overcome the top two Russians (the Hungarians had turned professional after winning the World title). But they both knew they would have to make a definite commitment to train full-time. Betty Callaway said she would not presume to ask Chris to give up his very promising career in the police force, but if they did decide to skate full-time she could arrange for them to practise under ideal conditions at the West German training centre at Oberstdorf. They really had no choice. They discussed the matter with their parents and came to the conclusion that they could manage to scrape by financially until the 1981 World Championship. If they had not found a sponsor by then, they would have to retire. They took every opportunity to publicise their need. When they won the St Ivel contest they smiled at the television camera with what they hoped were pleasantly pleading looks. They repeated the appeal after regaining their British title, but found no response.

They were in great demand, however, to give exhibitions. They jetted to Zagreb, then to Boston for a charity show, and gave up their Christmas to do exhibitions in Germany. They certainly weren't starving, but they weren't acquiring any money for their training expenses. (The ISU sets very stringent limits to the amount amateur skaters can receive for giving an exhibition; this was doubled in the summer of 1982.) They were beginning to despair when they heard that the Nottingham City Council had voted them a £7000 grant renewable after six months. Chris was amazed. He had almost neglected to submit their form, having felt they had no chance of success. Buoyed up by this marvellous news they proceeded to give the Council its money's worth right away. From the first compulsory dance in the 1981 European Championship in Innsbruck they skated and carried themselves like true champions.

After the first round it became obvious they would easily beat Natalia Linichuk and Gennadi Karponosov, the Olympic gold-medal winners who had won the World Championship in 1978 and 1979 and were defending their 1979 and 1980 European title. They were also clearly ahead of the legendary Min and Mo, European champions in 1977 and 1978. After this defeat Linichuk and Karponosov retired, but Min and Mo competed through to the 1982 Championships, after which they left competitive skating to start a family.

Jayne and Chris attribute most of their success to their increased training opportunities. When their Cha Cha OSP didn't have the desired effect on the St Ivel audience in September 1980, they had had time to change it. Since it sometimes takes them a whole day to devise ten seconds' worth of choreography, they would not have had the necessary time had they not been skating all day every day, sometimes for seven hours at one go.

They went on to show that the European victory was no fluke by winning the 1981 World Championship in Hartford, USA. Though unable to watch them compete because of their show commitments, Kristina and Andy travelled several hundred miles just to wish them good luck. Luck was something they did not need, so clearly were they superior to the other contestants. Only one aspect was missing: no sixes were awarded in that event.

After the month-long ISU tour of champions around the United States, they were asked what had been the highlight of the trip. Their complete devotion to skating was echoed in their reply. The places they had seen were nice but they had most enjoyed the opportunity to meet Britain's last World ice dance champion, Bernard Ford, who now teaches in Canada. And how had it felt to be fêted as World champions? Chris replied that as all the World champions were on the tour they didn't feel special. Official recognition that they were no longer an ordinary couple, however, came when the Queen made them MBEs. Chris dithered at first, bristling at the thought of wearing formal attire to accept the honour, but in the end he agreed to don a top hat and tails.

Their summer training was even more intense than before. For the previous season's free dance they had followed the normal policy of using four separate pieces of music to show that they could interpret different moods, and this was the plan they originally intended to use again. However, Chris discovered a piece of music in the Nottingham BBC Music Library which so pleased him, although he had got hold of only about forty seconds' worth of it, he set out to track it down. It was from an overture to a show which had flopped on Broadway after only nine performances in 1971. It took a lot of perseverance, but eventually he was able to obtain a record of the whole overture from the United States.

The juggling mime from 'Barnum on Ice'

Jayne and Chris's Rock and Roll exhibition

One of their most popular exhibition numbers was their Rhumba. Here Jayne and Chris bring out the very essence of this slinky, sensuous movement

Though Jayne liked this music she was completely set against using it for their whole four minutes, and it just didn't fit into any of their other selections. It took Chris some time to bring Jayne around to his way of thinking. The overture to *Mack and Mabel* grew on them to such a degree that the moves they choreographed were to reflect fairly accurately the story of the show although, at that time, they did not know the plot, which told of the Hollywood silent-film producer, Mack Sennett, and his stormy romance with his leading lady, Mabel Norman.

The piece was an immediate success. At its first showing in the St Ivel contest, three of the judges in the seven-member panel held up sixes for artistic impression. It was obvious what Jayne and Chris were attempting to show. Chris started out waving his arms as if swirling a cloak and Jayne reacted as if seeing a villain. There was a well-choreographed chase and struggle with entwined legs and complicated swift footwork, a train sequence, a reconciliation and romance section, and a happy ending. It was marvellous theatre but, as Betty Callaway pointed out, the most testing part was to maintain this aspect while making sure that the presentation contained the greatest amount of difficulty.

Six weeks later in the British championship 'Mack and Mabel' was rewarded with more sixes. Two of the nine judges, both of whom had never given a six before in their judging careers, gave them a six for both categories in the free dance. Five others gave a six for their second mark. It was a very emotional moment. By coincidence, a revival of *Mack and Mabel* was playing in Nottingham at that time. One of the musicians saw Jayne and Chris's performance on television and became convinced they had illegally taped the music from the show. He was astounded to discover they had found it themselves. Because Jayne and Chris made this music so popular, a record of the overture was issued and request programmes reported an astonishing demand for it.

They had also created a breathtakingly beautiful piece for their Blues OSP, using the lullaby 'Summertime' from the George Gershwin opera *Porgy and Bess*. At the end of their St Ivel presentation, when Chris bent over and Jayne stretched languidly over his back, her eyes slowly closing, there was absolute silence. Then tremendous applause broke out. There was more applause as the Russian judge held up a six. This programme, evoking so well the hot humidity and lethargy of the Louisiana lowlands, the inner tormented soul of the Blues, will remain etched on the memory.

Len Sayward, Chris's former coach, was amazed to discover his involvement with music. When he had partnered Sandra Elson he would not even venture an opinion on what music they should use. Betty explained part of Chris and Jayne's progress as coming from the freedom they now felt to express emotion in their skating. While Chris had been a policeman he was naturally reluctant to allow his feelings to show fully.

The 'Mack and Mabel' routine began with
Chris, as the villain, chasing the ingenue

The routine brought them a record number
of sixes

His proper British reserve held him back. Jayne didn't realise that it was necessary for her to act, not just to skate. Instead of concentrating on her feet it was essential for her to feel the music and react to it with all of her body. The chains that locked them into stereotyped roles of appropriate behaviour had been broken.

A short time after the British championship Jayne and Chris took their gold star test, the first time this NSA plum had been attempted, although it had been on the books for fifteen years. Coachloads of spectators descended on Nottingham to see them. Because of the numbers wanting to watch, an admission charge of 50p was made, the money being sent to charity. It was the first time anyone had paid to watch a test.

After all this excitement it would not be enough for Chris and Jayne simply to win the 1982 European Championship in Lyons, they had to gain sixes – and they did. They received first place from every judge in every portion of the Championship, and for their 'Summertime Blues' they were given three sixes. In the free dance they performed last. This meant that the judges felt freer to award sixes. Eight of the nine rewarded 'Mack and Mabel' with a six as the second mark and three of those judges, the French, Italian and Austrian, also gave it a six in the first set of marks. Only the bald-headed Russian, Igor Kabanov, refused to pull out a six. The number of sixes broke the record set by Irina Rodnina and Alexander Zaitsev in the 1973 European Championships.

Hordes of British supporters made plans to fly to Copenhagen to support Chris and Jayne that March as they defended their World title.

Torvill and Dean 27

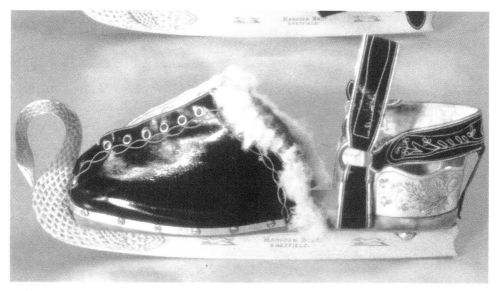

A skate belonging to Queen Victoria. The official historian of the NSA, Dennis Bird, has unearthed from Queen Victoria's personal journal her account of how she had saved Prince Albert's life when he fell through the ice while skating on the frozen lake at Buckingham Palace

Thin Ice, the second of Sonja Henie's twelve films, was made quickly to cash in on her appeal after the enormous success of *One in a Million* (page 43)

Ice dancers, including Diane Towler and Bernard Ford of Great Britain, gave exhibitions at the 1968 Grenoble Winter Olympics, hoping to get their sport accepted into the Olympic schedule though this did not happen until 1976 (page 48)

Janet Lynn, the most popular skater never to win a World Championship, won an Olympic bronze medal in 1972 and signed a professional contract for a huge amount of money in 1973. Here she demonstrates an outside spreadeagle (page 49)

For John Curry, skating was a substitute for ballet. He moved over the ice with marvellous smoothness and grace (page 51)

Even the compulsory dances, which are normally executed in an empty arena, were performed in front of several hundred spectators, almost all of whom appeared to be waving, or had clothing made out of, Union Jacks. They got their money's worth in the OSP. The French judge awarded Jayne and Chris a six for the first mark, and five judges gave them a six for the second mark – a record number for an OSP. On the Friday evening the nine o'clock news on BBC was delayed for forty minutes to show live ice dancing, with Robin Cousins commentating. Jayne and Chris followed their usual warm-up policy of skating apart. 'There's nothing you can practise from the programme,' Chris explained. 'All you can do is get the feel of the ice.'

They had drawn to skate first of the top five and the fans were worried that this would mean that the sixes would not appear. The tension in the arena was tangibly growing, and the applause when their names were called was almost deafening. The sound for television is fed through TV's own system, not picked up from the arena, so television audiences weren't aware that from the train sequence onwards to the point where Jayne caught her fingernail on Chris's waistcoat and undid it, the clapping had reached such a pitch that the music was completely drowned out. They knew the programme so well that they were able to continue, but the performance was not as perfect as in Lyons.

The first set of marks were all 5.9s. A hush settled over the capacity crowd as it readied itself to boo had no sixes flashed up on the electronic scoreboard for the second set. That was thwarted by five of the seven judges, none of whom was British. Adding together the scores of the OSP and the free dance, Jayne and Chris had scored eleven sixes in all and had broken another record. The most number of sixes awarded in a World Championship had previously been seven, given to Don Jackson of Canada for his performance in 1962.

Under normal conditions that would have been the last showing of 'Mack and Mabel'. The costumes of old gold would have been pushed to the back of the wardrobe and the music tapes lost in a drawer. The impact of the piece, however, was such that the fans refused to let it die. The Canadian Association was so insistent that Jayne and Chris come to the 1982 Skate Canada contest and perform it that they reluctantly agreed. No skaters have ever skated their full free routine as an exhibition before. Again Jayne and Chris were breaking new ground.

Their outfits were beginning to show wear. Jayne's gold feathers were shedding, and bald patches had to be repaired using hair lacquer for glue. Courtney Jones, who designs their costumes, had originally envisaged the outfits as champagne-coloured, to blend with their hair shades, but after initial reservations decided that gold was entirely appropriate. Many felt they were too showy. Those critics were even more dismayed at Chris and Jayne's costumes for their 1983 season's 'Barnum' routine.

The idea of presenting a circus atmosphere on ice had formed in Chris's mind before the end of the 1981–2 season. A few days after winning the 1982 World Championship they were in Moscow on the first stop of the ISU tour of champions. Chris swopped his Bolshoi Ballet ticket for one for the Moscow State Circus. Betty Callaway says she should have known that something was up, since she knows how much Chris enjoys watching the ballet. Later on in the tour, while in France, they heard some music from *Barnum*, the musical about the life of Phineas T. Barnum, who billed himself as the world's greatest showman. On their return they went to see the show at the London Palladium. The star Michael Crawford, peeping through the curtains, spotted them in the audience. He invited them backstage. They discussed with him their idea for basing their new routine on the *Barnum* theme, but one problem would be that they needed non-vocal music. Crawford thereupon set up a recording session with the musical director of the show. Many of the musicians donated their time, but the cost for the recording studios was substantial.

In the meantime Chris and Jayne had gone back to Oberstdorf with its three ice surfaces and boarding school in the Training Centre. None of the rinks in England are big enough to merit Olympic rating, another reason why the British champions spend so much of their time abroad. While there it was decided that Jayne should accompany Betty Callaway to the recording session back in England because, says Chris, she has the best musical ear. The session was supposed to last four hours but developed into an eleven-hour marathon. The whole process was very precise as each instrument was recorded individually. When completed, it was discovered that the music ran for four minutes and twelve seconds, two seconds over the allowed maximum. Then, when the tape was played in the ice rink it sounded entirely different, and some further changes had to be made. The total cost was £1500.

Unlike the 'Mack and Mabel' routine, Chris explained, the 'Barnum' programme did not tell a story, but sought to convey the joy circus performers have in their work and the delight audiences experience watching them. The routine was kept secret while Crawford helped Jayne and Chris develop circus business on Sundays on the stage of the Palladium. He even came to the Peterborough rink so that he could work with them on the ice. Among the many things he taught them was that there is a difference between juggling with three balls and with five. With five balls the eyes go higher. Jayne decided that miming three balls would be quite enough. One thing they had to insist on was that Michael call Mrs Callaway anything but Betty. Every time he did so, he would revert to the character he played in the television series *Some Mothers do 'ave 'em*. They would collapse in hysteria, and no work would get done. In the end they decided he should call her Henry.

Anna Kondrashova just misses the spotlight in an exhibition (page 54)

Claudia Leistner, seen in a spiral, was formerly a competitive roller skater (page 54)

Elena Vodorezova finishing her exhibition with a flourish (page 54)

Katarina Witt, the 1983 European champion, performs a pull-up camel spin (page 71)

Jayne and Chris express intense emotion in a Rhumba exhibition

The routine, finally unveiled in the British championship, was extremely well received, but was given only one six because Jayne's hand slipped on Chris's costume, destroying the image of perfection. Several items in the routine were immediately obvious. Some were more subtle, and it took a second viewing to appreciate them. The initial impressions given were of rolling out the elephant drums, the clown putting on make-up, juggling, the swinging trapeze, the sliding trombones, and balancing on a high wire – the point where Jayne collapsed into Chris's arms.

The interest in Jayne and Chris by now was such that Trud, the Russian news agency, even sent a man to Nottingham to cover the British championship, something that had never happened before. Their white outfits caused a lot of consternation amongst the ice dance officials, as Courtney Jones had feared. White is always a problem because all too easily undergarments can show through. Extra care was taken to make sure this wouldn't happen. The designs that Courtney dreams up for Jayne are given to Sylvia Parish who makes up all her skating outfits. Because the ISU restrictions on lifts in amateur ice dancing were eased in the summer of 1982, Chris was now free to throw Jayne over his shoulder, which placed extra strain on her outfits. When her dress was found to be pulling at the shoulder a new one was made for the World

Championships with the zip at the side instead of the front. Chris's costumes are made up by Ron Gunn who has the ability to produce clothes in which the collar stays down even when the arms are raised, and can make the outfit tight enough so that the line looks elegant without constricting any movement.

Not only were their white outfits thought too professional for amateurs, their 'Barnum' routine was criticised for containing too much mime, and the music seemed less catchy than 'Mack and Mabel'. Some officials also criticised their OSP and their treatment of the compulsories. These had been executed with absolutely unflawed technique. However, Jayne and Chris had experimented with arm positions in the Argentine Tango and the Ravensburger Waltz. In itself, this would not have been too revolutionary but, in trying to breathe some life into these dull pieces, in which all the steps are exactly specified and performed to one of three pieces of music chosen by the ISU, they did not repeat the same arm variation in each of the three sequences. To be fair, the critics voiced their doubts because they feared that these innovations would provide other countries' judges with a reason to mark them down. They knew the Russian judge would be looking for any excuse.

The OSP was the Rock and Roll, and Jayne and Chris had picked music from the finale of the show, *Song and Dance*, which has music by Andrew Lloyd Webber based on a Theme and Variations by Paganini. They had gone to see this show without expecting it to contain any music they would be able to use. However, at the finale when the dancers' energetic gyrations overwhelm the stage, they looked wordlessly at each other. They knew this was for them.

The ISU had produced a many-paged leaflet detailing what could and could not be used in the Rock and Roll number. There were to be no lifts, and only certain holds could be used. Unfortunately this put a damper on many couples' imaginations, and this section did not turn out to be as exciting as had been hoped. Too many couples took one look at all the restrictions and confined themselves to shaking their heads and waving their arms. Jayne and Chris refused to be discouraged. After much trial and error, and a lot of wasted time, they designed two moves which fitted all the limitations – variations on the lateral twists executed by pair skaters, but done with Jayne spread out horizontally at Chris's feet.

Most expert reaction to these lateral twists was one of disbelief, followed by a puzzled muttering. The World professional ice dance champion, Juri Musil, was one who openly stated that the moves were plainly impossible. The OSP was so difficult that, while people deemed it a privilege to have been in Nottingham to witness this first showing, they weren't mesmerised as they had been by the 'Summertime Blues'. The feeling was more of astonishment. When news came later of Jayne's injury which was to keep them out of the European Championship, many said they weren't surprised. Chris and Jayne were pushing back the frontiers too fast and getting sucked into dangerous territory.

In Oberstdorf in January Chris and Jayne decided to work on a new lift for the start of the 'Barnum' routine. This would provide an even greater surprise for the audience. It was a 'levitation' lift in which Jayne would appear to be momentarily suspended five feet in the air and parallel to the ice. Chris tripped on the move and Jayne slammed heavily down, injuring her shoulder badly. They tried to continue practising but the shoulder was reinjured. Jayne had to take time off the ice and they had to withdraw from the forthcoming European event.

The organisers figured it cost them 6500 spectators for the final of the free dance. Because they have done so much of their training in Oberstdorf, the Germans have come to think of Chris and Jayne as their own. Near to Dortmund, the site of the contest, is a British Army base and the throngs of soldiers and their families who flooded to see Robin Cousins in 1980 were expected to follow them, too. It is fortunate that the injury occurred while they were in Oberstdorf because the Bavarian village has a sports clinic which is the envy of most countries. Mainly they treat skiers, but Jayne's injury was of a type which might have occurred to a skier, and they knew exactly what to do. After a course of extensive physiotherapy Jayne returned to training at the time of the European Championships with her shoulder bandaged, but could only do the compulsories. There were parts of the OSP they did not dare try. Betty Callaway was optimistic

When another top-level couple tried to copy this cartwheel the woman ended on her head

The projection of inner feelings came more easily to Chris than to Jayne

that they would be back in shape in time for the World Championships, but the more one heard about the injury the more serious it sounded.

The organisers of the European Championships gave Jayne and Chris their 'Most Unlucky Skater' award. Chris was given a very heavy metal sculpture of a Good Luck sign, while Jayne received a specially minted gold two pfennig piece. Whatever the fillip it gave them, they were at Helsinki for the World Championships. And so was Michael Crawford. *Barnum* had closed on 5 February after running longer than any other show in the seventy-year history of the London Palladium, and Michael took the opportunity to lend moral support to the British champions. Every practice was a show, spectators crowding into the arena as Jayne and Chris took the ice. Betty Callaway had anticipated this interest and had arranged for special practice outfits to help enhance the image they were trying to project. For instance, for their Rock and Roll number, both their practice and their competition outfits had their first initials appliquéd on, just as teenage clothes had in the fifties.

From the first compulsory in the competition proper, at 9 am on 9 March 1983, it was apparent that, however bad Jayne's shoulder had been, she could still perform like a champion. They were drawn to skate thirteenth, which meant that because of the draw rotation they were first on for the third compulsory, the Argentine Tango. The nine judges looked at their snooty, sultry dance and presented them with a straight line of 5.9s, the highest marks ever given for a compulsory. No one has ever received a six for a compulsory dance, but afterwards one of the judges confided that, had they skated this dance last, he would have awarded them a six, their technique had been so magnificent.

The next day their OSP was rewarded with one six in the first set and six in the second, which meant they had broken their own record, established the previous year. There was one anxious moment when Chris caught his hand in Jayne's voluminous but short skirt in the extremely difficult lateral twist. Chris shrugged off the sixes. 'There's nothing to say when everything goes all right.'

The free dance final, shown live by BBC on Saturday afternoon, had millions glued to their television sets. Once again Robin Cousins aided Alan Weeks's commentary. This year, growing more confident with experience, Robin went as far as to air some people's criticism that Jayne and Chris were breaking the rules of ice dancing. The panel of judges disagreed. They awarded 'Barnum on Ice' straight 5.9s for the first mark and straight sixes for the second. This was another peak; never before had a complete row of sixes been given in an international championship. Irina Rodnina and Alexander Zaitsev scored eight out of nine sixes in the European Championship short programme in 1973 for their second set of marks. They also gained sixes in their first set, but not as many as Chris and Jayne were given for their OSP.

Jayne cried as the Union Jack was raised to celebrate their third World victory. The euphoria lasted only as long as they were on the rostrum. The next morning they were almost miserable because they were not being left alone to get going on the ideas which just tumble out. They had already decided on a possible theme for the Olympic year, but needed time together to see if it was feasible.

In October this remarkable couple came up with another first. They performed a nine minute fifty-eight second exhibition interpreting Richard Rodger's *Slaughter on Tenth Avenue* for a gala at the Queens ice club. No skaters have kept a crowd mesmerised for over five minutes before. Their effort was so intense that Betty Callaway said she didn't know whether it would be repeated. Fortunately, television cameras have recorded these moments for posterity.

Jayne and Chris have made it clear that after the Winter Olympic Games at Sarajevo they will retire to give professional exhibitions, but not in a conventional type of ice show. Eventually they want to teach, and Chris would like to see a training centre built in Nottingham to match the one at Oberstdorf where they have spent so many fruitful and enjoyable hours.

Their Rock and Roll in 1983 earned them an unprecedented number of sixes for the OSP

2

The World's Greatest Skaters
Yesterday and today

From earliest times people have enjoyed the thrill of sliding on frozen water, as careless to the dangers as was St Lidwina, the sport's patron saint. She broke at least one rib while skating on a canal in Holland in 1396 when she was fifteen and was permanently invalided as a result. The rest of her life, thirty-seven years, was spent performing good works and several miracles from her bedside. Her bones are buried in Scheidam and some believed they protected the town from bombing during the Second World War.

John Curry, the 1976 Olympic champion, cheerfully ignored his father's warnings of how the surface might give way, plunging him into the chilling depths when he took to the ice on a Christmas holiday in the Fens. The boy's enthusiasm was undaunted, but when his mother saw him wading through the mush at the side of the pond on his way to firmer ice, she laid down the law. Any skating was to be done on artificial ice.

It was the British who formed the world's first skating club. The exact date is uncertain, but the Edinburgh Skating Club is believed to have come into being around 1650. At this time applicants for membership had to skate a circle first on one foot, then on the other, and finally jump over three top hats piled on top of each other. The club existed until 1966. In 1830 an organisation simply called The Skating Club was formed in London. Here the English style was developed. While skaters in other countries were content to draw their names on the ice or make elaborate figures resembling flowers with the tracings left by their skates, the English developed a more social, if formal, activity, a kind of square dancing without music. Four skaters were arranged around an orange and a caller would shout out the moves. On the caller's instructions the skaters would turn, skate towards the orange, and away from it.

The first skating club in North America – the Philadelphia Skating Club and Humane Society – was founded in 1849. Such were the dangers of drowning that even today its members are required to carry a reel and coil of rope when skating outdoors, or be subject to a fine. Then, from New York, in the 1860s came the man who was to revolutionise skating

The British were always at the forefront in figure skating, as shown by this photo taken in 1910

and serve a death blow to the English style. Jackson Haines was a ballet master who designed his own skates and translated his art onto the ice, developing spirals from ballet's arabesques, spreadeagles from ballet's second position, and devising the sit spin.

Although Haines won the first two unofficial American championships in 1863 and 1864, his countrymen in general were lukewarm to his innovations. He decided to leave his wife and three children to seek fame in Europe. The British, too, were unreceptive to his performance but in Vienna he won instant success. Skating to the music that Johann Strauss had just composed, Haines took the city by storm. He made up waltzes, marches, mazurkas and quadrilles, adding to ballroom dancing a heady speed and pleasing grace, and founding the disciplines of ice dancing and pair skating. For eleven years he was feted throughout Austria, Hungary, Germany, Russia and Scandinavia. In 1876 he decided to return home. Travelling to Stockholm from St Petersburg, where he had given lessons to Tsar Alexander II, he was caught in an unexpected snowstorm while in a sleigh. He contracted pneumonia and died, aged thirty-six.

The first international skating meet was organised by the Viennese in 1882 and consisted of twenty-three prescribed school figures, a special figure chosen by the competitor, and a four-minute free-skating routine. Austrians took the first two places but third was Axel Paulsen of Norway whose name still lives on in the $1\frac{1}{2}$ rotation jump he invented, the axel.

The world's first rink using an artificially-made ice surface had opened in 1876. The Glaciarium in Chelsea used a process patented by John Gamgee, who also invented the slot machine. His freezing process was intended originally to preserve meat on the long sea voyage to Australia. It worked by pumping a mixture of ether, glycerine and brine through copper piping. Previous ventures in making artificial ice had been disastrous. An 1843 issue of *Punch* describes a visit to a rink near Baker Street where the ice was made not of frozen water but of a slush of chemicals including hog's lard and melted sulphur, which smelled abominably. Another attempt in Manchester required patrons to skate on an uneven surface through an extremely thick mist.

The success of the Chelsea rink spawned many others. The much larger Southport Glaciarium, 164 feet by 64 feet, opened in 1879, coinciding with the birth of the NSA, and remained open for ten years. Almost immediately rinks sprang up in other countries, and many more opened in Britain. The rink which was built in Charing Cross in 1893 was deemed adequate to hold the ISU's third competition in 1898. In 1924 these annual events were retrospectively named World Championships although only a handful of competitors had taken part.

In 1901 the ISU was shocked to receive an application for the following year's event from a British woman, Madge Syers-Cave. There were no regulations to deny her entry and she was placed second out of four behind the great Ulrich Salchow, who won the second of his ten world titles and is remembered as the inventor of the salchow jump. Some said she would have won had she not been a woman. The rules were quickly changed to exclude women, and a separate event for them was set up in 1906. Syers-Cave won the first two such competitions, as well as the Olympic gold medal in women's skating at the 1908 (Summer) Olympic Games in London. Women continued to compete with men in the British national championship until the 1930s.

Skating was also part of the 1920 (Summer) Olympic Games held in Antwerp. In that event the American Theresa Weld was warned by a judge, who considered it unfeminine, that she would be penalised if she insisted on jumping. She persisted in doing a small salchow jump, and won the free-skating portion and the bronze medal in a field of six competitors. The first Winter Olympic Games were set up in 1924 and held in Chamonix. Gillis Grafstrom of Sweden, an extremely graceful skater who gave the world the change foot sit spin and the jump sit spin, won the men's event and the second of his three Olympic gold medals.

The 1924 Winter Olympic Games are remembered as the start of a revolution sparked off by a pudgy, blonde-haired, blue-eyed eleven-year-old from Norway, Sonja Henie. Figure skating was then the province of a small, privileged, rich aristocracy. All participants were adults. As in so many Olympic Games that followed, the weather at Chamonix had proved a problem, with rain and sleet putting the big rink out of action. One day all the contestants, about thirty speed skaters, fifty figure skaters, and the ice hockey players, were crowded into the curling rink which measured 50 yards by 15 yards. Sonja, in a very short, fur-trimmed outfit, literally pushed her way through this august gathering and did a jump into a sit spin – to everyone's immense consternation. Because she was a child Sonja could wear knee-length skirts, in contrast to the older women's voluminous, ankle-length skirts, and this enabled her to try moves previously attempted only by men. All the same, Sonja finished eighth and last, although one of the seven judges in the free skating put her in first place with the champion, Herma Plank-Szabo.

Plank-Szabo had won the World title since the Championships resumed in 1922 after the First World War. Within two years Henie had won the silver medal behind her and in 1927, amidst great controversy, she took the title away from the Austrian. In those days each judge represented an individual club rather than a country. In 1927 there were one German, one Austrian and three Norwegian officials. How could these last not vote for their national champion as she delighted the capacity audience, including the king and queen, at the Frogner stadium in Oslo? The other officials complained and the present ruling of one judge per country was brought in shortly afterwards. In her autobiography, *Wings on My Feet*, Sonja claimed she suggested a reskate in London, but Plank-Szabo would not accept, and never competed again.

Sonja was unbeaten for the next ten years and her influence changed whole aspects of the sport. After her first tube-shaped dresses, she took

The great Sonja Henie won ten consecutive World titles and three Olympic gold medals

Cecilia Colledge of London, the 1937 World champion

to wearing circular skirts with a beige lining, beige bloomers, and matching beige boots instead of the traditional black boots. When everyone had copied this style, she turned to white boots, which are now universal for women, and shorter and shorter skirts. Her outfits were designed by some of Europe's finest couturiers. The popularity of the sport increased and the number of her competitors grew steadily. In the Winter Olympic Games at Lake Placid in 1932 two British eleven-year-olds, Megan Taylor and Cecilia Colledge, made effective starts to their international careers by gaining seventh and eighth places, and repeating these standings at the World Championships which followed in Montreal, in which fourteen women took part.

Megan's father taught skating, but Cecilia was inspired to ask her mother if she could try the sport after seeing Sonja win her second World title in 1928 in London. When Cecilia competed in Lake Placid she was eight months younger than Sonja had been in Chamonix in 1924, and she still holds the record as the youngest entrant in the Winter Olympic Games. Megan and Cecilia formed half the British team in the 1932 Olympics. The other two members were also figure skaters. One of them, fifteen-year-old Mollie Phillips, became the first woman to carry the British flag at the Olympics and, in 1947, continued her pioneering path by being appointed the first woman international judge (they had previously been deemed too frail to endure the rigours of officiating outdoors).

Meanwhile, Sonja Henie's spectacular career continued, astutely managed by her father. In those days, before the emergence of professional ice shows, clubs organised carnivals that starred leading amateurs and were extremely popular. Sonja developed a skill for becoming fatigued before her scheduled spots, unless consoled by a suitable present. Some of these were considerable. The Norwegian-American Society gave her a sports car. In 1947, after Barbara Ann Scott returned home as the first Canadian to win a World title, she was also given a car. Avery Brundage, the head of the International Olympic Committee (IOC), threatened to take away her amateur status unless she returned it. In vain she argued that Sonja had not been similarly threatened. In the end the car was temporarily returned for the few months it took the Canadian to win the Olympic gold medal, a compromise that foreshadowed the trust funds which can now be set up for athletes.

In the 1936 Olympics Cecilia Colledge came very close to toppling Sonja. The young Briton had been placed a close second in the school figures and could do technically more advanced moves than the Norwegian in the free skating. These were the days before the draws were made in sections to ensure that the top skaters always perform at the end of the proceedings. Cecilia drew to skate second of the twenty-three competitors, before some of the audience had even arrived, and her chance of winning slipped away when she fell. Sonja, skating last, enchanted the capacity crowd, which included Hitler, at the open-air Garmisch-Partenkirchen arena. Spotlights were turned on to augment the fading light and enhance her appeal. Nowadays a rule specifies that the lighting must remain the same for all contestants.

In 1936 Sonja and her father packed her gold medals from three consecutive Olympics and ten World Championships and headed for America. They hired a Los Angeles rink, put on a show and invited all the celebrities to whom they could gain access. Carole Lombard, Jeannette MacDonald, Ginger Rogers, Bette Davis, Gary Cooper, Mary Pickford, Douglas Fairbanks and John Barrymore were amongst the stars who turned up to see her skate, but not the one man they wanted in the audience – Darryl F. Zanuck. They had almost to kidnap the head of Twentieth Century-Fox to get him there, and even then he initially offered Sonja only a small role in one of his films. It took time, but they did persuade him to make a film built around her talents.

Sonja made twelve films in all, beautifully costumed and with specially-composed music, including 'Chatanooga Choo Choo', written for her seventh film, *Sun Valley Serenade*. The last, *Sonja Henie comes to London*, was filmed in the late 1950s. In all her films Sonja co-starred with well-known, bankable actors and they were enormous successes. As a result there was a boom in ice-rink manufacture to meet the demand of mothers trying to turn their daughters into skating stars. When Sonja died in 1969 her assets were worth many millions of pounds. Just outside her birthplace, Oslo, she created an art centre, and it is there that all her trophies are housed.

Etsuko Inada, a tiny eleven-year-old, the first woman to compete internationally for Japan, skated in the 1936 Olympics and might have starred in the 1940 event scheduled for Sapporo in her home country, had war not broken out. The hostilities almost certainly deprived Britain of victories in Sapporo. Two Britons, Graham Sharp and Freddie Tomlins, had gained first and second places in the men's singles event in the 1939 World Championships, while the rivalry continued between Cecilia Colledge, who had won the 1937 World title, and Megan Taylor, who captured it in 1938 and 1939. Closing the ranks behind them was another Briton, fourteen-year-old Daphne Walker, who won bronze medals in the 1939 European and World Championships.

It was not surprising that North Americans, whose skating activities had not been interrupted during the war, should do well when the sport resumed in 1947. When Eva Pawlik of Austria unsuccessfully challenged Barbara Ann Scott in 1948 one reason given for her failure was that she skated with dirty boots and holes in her tights. The boots were so old they no longer responded to cleaning and the holes were darned. It was the best she could manage with all the shortages in her country.

Dick Button who won the men's event that year was a superb free skater, dazzling spectators with jumps that were clearly higher than any that had been seen before. He attributes part of his 1948 European Championship success to a squeegee mop. When it was his turn to do the fifth figure, the back paragraph loops, the ice was extremely wet in the one desirable part of this outdoor rink which did not have a bumpy surface. Just as he was about to give in and choose another spot, he saw the mop, swept away the water, and gained high marks for the figure.

Button dominated the sport until 1952, developing moves such as the double axel, the flying camel, and executing the world's first triple jump. Most skaters give credit to their teachers and Button was no exception. If Gus Lussi had ordered him to jump through a window, Button later said, he would have done so, and he would have been sure to point his feet and hold his head high as Lussi had instructed. Lussi was not a former competitive skater but a ski jumper who applied the theories of that sport to the ice.

The epitome of quiet British reserve, Jeannette Altwegg from Liverpool, was crowned queen to Button's king in the 1952 Olympics. Floating to an Olympic victory on her unmatched ability to draw geometrically perfect circles on the ice, the former tennis champion had moved up a place each year in the World Championship, after being fifth in 1947, to win it in 1951. In 1952, before the Olympics, she defended her European title but turned down the chance to skate for the few extra weeks after her Olympic success that were needed to defend her World title. Instead she

Dick Button, who won gold medals in the 1948 and 1952 Olympics and was the first to accomplish a triple rotation jump, was known for the amazing height of his jumps

took up a job as a house mother for refugee children in the Pestalozzi village in Switzerland. Her nominal salary was contrasted at the time with the various offers that had been made to her to skate professionally. Her selflessness later earned her the CBE.

The following year a brother and sister team, John and Jennifer Nicks from Brighton, captured the World pair title, though film of that event shows it hardly resembled today's dazzling and daring contests. Both partners later became teachers in North America, as did Cecilia Colledge and Megan Taylor.

The early 1950s were an exceptionally good period for British skating. Ice dancing was accepted into the World championship schedule in 1952 and only one non-British couple claimed the title until 1970. The first four were won by Jean Westwood and Lawrence Demmy, although at home they were consistently beaten by the less showy but technically more skilful Joan Dewhirst and John Slater. The latter's son, Nicky, with his partner, Karen Barber, is expected to win the British title after Jayne Torvill and Christopher Dean turn professional.

Courtney Jones, who was to win five British and European Championships and four World titles, was originally a pair skater and started competing as an ice dancer almost casually. He was scheduled to take his gold ice dance test at the Queens rink with his instructor, Gladys Hogg. She fell ill and suggested he take as his partner for the test another pupil of hers, June Markham. They did so well that they entered a competition and did better than expected. Three weeks later they were runners-up for the British title and shortly afterwards gained the second place in the

Courtney Jones, who designs all Torvill and Dean's outfits, seen here with June Markham with whom he won the first two of his four World titles

Joan Dewhirst and John Slater, British champions in 1951–3, were beaten for the World title by the flashier Jean Westwood and Lawrence Demmy.

1956 European and World Championships, events which they won in the two succeeding years. When Markham retired, Jones found another partner, Doreen Denny, with whom to claim the top awards. The tragic airplane crash which wiped out the entire US team on its way to the 1961 World Championships and led to the cancellation of the event denied him his fifth World title.

In 1953 Tenley Albright became the first American woman to win a World title. She won it again in 1955 and also won the 1956 Olympic gold medal. After qualifying as a surgeon, she was the first woman invited to become a member of the IOC. Her successor as World and Olympic champion was another American, Carol Heiss, who won the World title five times from 1956 to 1960. She later married Hayes Alan Jenkins, who had proved unbeatable from 1953–6, and whose younger brother, David, was to be equally invincible from 1957–60.

Sjoukje Dijkstra, from Holland, won the silver medal in the 1960 Winter Olympic Games in Squaw Valley and was runner-up to Heiss at theWorld Championship that year. She was not seriously challenged for the following four years. After winning the Olympic crown in 1964 she joined an ice show at an enormous salary. It was a spectacular achievement for a skater who, as a ten-year-old, had been nearly dismissed as untalented.

Throughout this era keen spectators were at the side of the rink during every competition, filming the proceedings. Learning from their shots, the Soviets were about to begin their climb to the top of the skating world. The first category in which they demonstrated success was the pairs, in which a Moscow husband and wife team, Nina and Stanislav Zhuk, won silver medals at the 1958 and 1959 European Championships. They were supplanted by a couple who were to capture the imagination of television viewers all over the world, Ludmila Belousova and Oleg Protopopov. Their first success came in the 1964 Olympics in Innsbruck

The ice flakes spray up as four World champions perform a hockey stop at Richmond ice rink in 1962. Maria and Otto Jelinek (left), Canada, had won the pairs championship in Prague that year. Don Jackson (right), Canada, had won the men's title with the first triple lutz jump. Sjoukje Dijkstra (second from right), Holland, was the only one of the four to continue as an amateur, going on to win Olympic gold in 1964

The Protopopovs, after they had defected to the West, demonstrating the forward inside death spiral, a move they invented for the 1969 season

when they won the gold medals in a very tight decision over Marika Kilius and Hans Jurgen Baumler of West Germany.

In 1969 the Protopopovs in their turn were dethroned by Irina Rodnina and Alexei Ulanov, a couple developed by Stanislav Zhuk who realised that the Protopopovs' grace could not be surpassed and chose to eclipse them with pyrotechnics. Rodnina and Ulanov did combinations of jumps never seen in a pairs event and dazzled the spectators with their speed. When the Protopopovs returned home to Leningrad they were told to retire by their Moscow-based Association. They declined and found they could only obtain ice time from midnight to two or three in the morning – and that only through the intervention of a friend. Protopopov later recalled that their names disappeared from the newspapers and each year they fell lower in the national standings.

They had hoped to take part in the 1972 Olympics. When that wasn't possible they managed, through Dick Button who was now presenting skating events for television, to take part in and win a professional invitation contest in Japan in December 1972. Back home, it took them nine months and the help of an important government official to get a job in Leningrad's ice show. Even then their names were not included in the programme. By 1978 they realised their 'souls were being drained away'. Protopopov scorned becoming a teacher, the only path open to him. He said they wanted him to stand by the barrier for eighty kopeks an hour, shouting 'C'mon. C'mon.' The couple defected in 1979. After skating with an American show, 'Ice Capades', for a season, they now live in Switzerland. He has a dream of getting together enough money to make a six-hour epic film about skating.

First with Ulanov, and then with Alexander Zaitsev, Rodnina won ten consecutive World Championships and three Olympic gold medals, a record that matches Sonja Henie's. Russian skaters were soon to take top honours in ice dancing, too. Ludmila Pakhomova and her original partner, Viktor Rishkin, were the first Russians to enter a World ice dance championship. Although they did poorly in the compulsory dance section of the 1966 event they finished tenth out of sixteen after improving their standing with an expressive free dance. Rishkin appeared with a different partner the following year, and meanwhile Pakhomova had teamed up with Alexander Gorshkov, who was to become her husband. In 1968 the two Russian ice dance couples came fifth and sixth in the World event. To everyone's surprise, the following year Pakhomova and Gorshkov took second place behind Britain's Diane Towler and Bernard Ford, who were winning their fourth, and last, World title.

Pakhomova was extremely energetic and possessed a charisma that made judges overlook Gorshkov's obvious faults. He was a far inferior skater. However, in 1970 they won the title in a close decision over the US champions, Judy Schwomeyer and James Sladky. Mollie Phillips, the British judge, sided with the four judges from the Communist bloc against the other four judges. After that they continued to improve. Apart from an upset in the 1972 European Championship, and Gorshkov's illness which prevented them taking part in the 1975 World Championship, they won everything up to 1976 including the first Olympic gold medals ever awarded for ice dance.

Towler and Ford had had an even more meteoric rise to fame. She was a sophisticated Londoner; he was a boy from Birmingham who came intermittently to the Queens Ice Club to take instructions from the doyenne of skating instructors, Gladys Hogg. She sensed that they would do well together but Diane was extremely apprehensive.

Together they created magic. In their first World Championship in 1964 they were thirteenth out of sixteen. The following year the title was theirs. They were inventive and fast, and their routine to music from the film *Zorba the Greek* will always remain in the memory. Some of their innovations were by no means universally approved. At the national championship in November 1968 their bright orange outfits with a military design were thought too flashy. Officials were also shocked that they had chosen to wear boot covers of the same material – something considered suitable only for professionals. They were told in no uncertain terms that their costumes would have to be more subdued for their international appearances – hard to believe these days when nearly all skaters wear boot covers to extend the line of their outfits.

The Sabena plane disaster in Brussels in 1961 not only wiped out the entire American skating team; it took the lives of the leading US coaches. Carlo Fassi of Italy, who had won the 1953 and 1954 European Championships, was invited to fill one of these tragic gaps. His first famous pupil was Peggy Fleming, who came to him having twice won the US title and a bronze medal in the 1965 World Championship. She was said to combine steel and crystal with a soft flow over the ice. In 1966 she dethroned the World champion, Petra Burka of Canada, who had lost her strength along with many pounds in a weight reduction programme.

Fleming did not skate her best in the 1968 Winter Olympics at Grenoble, despite winning. Errors included a last-minute substitution of a single axel for a double and an underrotated double lutz. Fassi blamed Mrs Fleming, a notorious stage mother. He said it was the first time the daughter had not taken the ice immediately after a row with her mother, and normally that appeared to increase Peggy's competitive spirit. It was the worst performance she had given in the four and a half years he'd been coaching her.

Fleming's successor as US champion, a title she claimed five times, was Janet Lynn, the blonde pixie with the glowing smile, who delighted the world with her beautiful free skating but never won a World Championship. She had started skating as a pathologically shy youngster and by the age of seven was showing such promise that her family dropped her last name, Nowicki, so that the public would not have to contend with such a mouthful, and lightened her mousy coloured hair.

In 1975 Sergei Volkov from Leningrad became the first Russian to win the men's World Championship but after he failed to win a medal in

Peggy Fleming in an outside spread. She would take off from this position into a double axel jump and resume it on landing – a feat that has been rarely repeated

John Curry in the outfit he made so familiar. Here he has skated forward, risen onto his toe rake and will, in a seemingly impossible move, start to move backwards

either the 1976 European Championship or the Olympic Games, he was pulled out of the World team and not allowed to defend his title.

The 1976 season belonged to John Curry. After the free skating at the European Championship in Geneva there was no doubt in the spectators' minds that he was the champion. He had skated superlatively. However, before the event his coach, Carlo Fassi, had advised him to withdraw. With five judges from behind the Iron Curtain and only four from the West, Fassi could not see how the Briton would win. He was right to worry. Had the Czech judge not sided with Curry against the other four Communist judges who voted for the Russian, Vladimir Kovalev, Curry would have been placed second. The Czech judge has not judged outside his country since then.

Curry skated equally well to win the gold in a memorable performance at the Innsbruck Olympics. Here the decision was far clearer, although the Russian judge still voted for Kovalev and the Canadian judge for Toller Cranston. Both judges were suspended for showing national bias. (In 1977, because the repeated suspensions of individual Russian judges did not seem to be having a corrective action, the ISU took the unprecedented step of banning all Russian judges from taking part in the international championships for the 1978 season. Even so, national bias is still a problem.) Despite a lay-off of ten days, Curry then made a last-minute decision to try for the grand slam at the World Championship at Göteborg. The time away from the ice told on his school figures, and he also made an error in his short programme. Nevertheless his free skating, to Minkus's ballet music *Don Quixote*, was magnificent, and he won that title to complete the hat trick.

Even at an early age Curry showed an unusual awareness of line. He remembers that the first routine he devised consisted mostly of spirals, like this one here, and was set to a piece of music called 'The Swallows'

John Curry executes a stag jump. He says this is his favourite photograph

For the 26-year-old from Birmingham it had been a long road to the top. As a child he had wanted to be a ballet dancer. His father would not agree, and Curry started skating as a substitute. His father accidentally shot himself in a hotel room when John was sixteen, and he moved to London at that point to train with Arnold Gerschwiler, the Richmond coach. He was a strict disciplinarian and the association was a hard one for Curry. His main joy was that he could now begin ballet classes. Although John always moved over the ice with a wonderful feline grace and awareness of line, he had problems with jumps. He skated so badly at the 1971 World Championship in Lyons that he dreaded facing Gerschwiler, and left the ice by a side-entrance. He won a bronze medal in the European Championship in 1974, but was ready to give up everything after making a mess of the World event that year. There, in Munich, an American said he'd like to help. Curry thought the man was about to give him advice on his jumping, but he wanted to sponsor Curry and bring him to the United States. Ed Mosler, the heir to the Mosler Safe fortune, has sponsored many athletes including most of the US team. Curry is the only non-American he has helped.

Initially Curry had hoped to train with Janet Lynn's coach, Slavka Kahout, but she had married Dick Button and, with a child to look after, was not interested in teaching. He followed her advice, though, that he go first to Gus Lussi to get his jumping straightened out and then to Fassi but it was not until after he had taken the est course of positive thinking in the autumn of 1975 that he realised his full capability and soared right to the top. His performance in Innsbruck undoubtedly deserved a string of

John Curry and the American Jo Jo Starbuck perform their famous Tango routine

Robin Cousins demonstrates an inside spreadeagle

sixes, but he had drawn to skate first of the top six, and no judge was prepared to give the maximum at that stage.

Curry's wins focused attention on the boy who would obviously succeed him as British champion, Robin Cousins. Like Curry, Cousins's first love was the ballet and he was offered a scholarship to the Royal School of Ballet which he turned down to concentrate on skating. He might never have skated at all had the family not taken a summer holiday in Bournemouth. Fred Cousins took Robin's two older brothers to the beach, but his mother took him with her to look around the shops. They passed the ice rink and, since it was very hot, she thought it would be nice to go inside. She asked a passing stranger on the ice if he could help Robin and, much to her chagrin, found she had bumped into an instructor. He marched her to the desk and explained how much a lesson would be. It was a hefty slice out of that day's budget but she was too embarrassed to retreat. With his dance training Robin did so well that the instructor could not believe he had never been on skates before.

A rink opened soon afterwards in Cousins's hometown of Bristol and he started to take lessons. Once he started private coaching with Pam Davies he made rapid progress, winning the 1970 British primary championship and the 1972 British junior championship. Already his pattern of performance was set – a win after being placed last in the school figures section. As junior champion he was allowed to enter the senior event, and because he was placed third in this gained a place on the team for the 1973 European Championship. Film of this event shows that the height of his jumps was already impressive, but he was still very unpolished.

Now he came to London to train with Gladys Hogg – the start of a very lonely period for the fifteen-year-old, travelling up to London on Monday morning and back to Bristol on Friday afternoon. There were always his skating goals, however. In John Curry's last national championship he fell, enabling a delighted Cousins to win the free-skating section, thereby achieving one goal. Nevertheless, in the Olympics, while Curry shone gloriously bright, Cousins was completely overlooked. One German journalist wrote that Cousins skated to 'Three Blind Mice' in front of nine blind judges. A few months later Cousins gained his first international success when he won the St Gervais Grand Prix in France. This event had been Curry's first and only international win before the 1976 season.

That December, as British champion and looking forward to competing at world level as a worthy successor to Curry, Cousins tore a knee cartilage and had to have an operation. Determined not to lose that season because of the injury, he devised with his family a special apparatus to exercise the affected muscles and learned to do his required elements on his other leg. He was bitterly hurt by talk that he just wanted to go for

Robin Cousins showing a magnificent Russian split at the Arosa rink, Richmond, not long before he won his Olympic gold medal

the trip to the World Championships in Tokyo and would pull out of the event immediately he got there. Robin was lying sixth as he went into the free skating, determined not to quit in spite of agonising pain. However, it was obvious halfway through his routine that his knee had gone completely and, to his great distress, he had to abandon his efforts.

Gladys Hogg does not travel by plane, and so Cousins was looked after in Japan by Fassi and his wife, Christa. As a result he decided to follow Curry's example and train in Denver with them. He adapted to his new life extremely well. There were other boys at the rink of comparable ability, including Scott Hamilton who was to win his first World Championship in 1981, and their efforts kept Cousins on his toes and made it easier to get through the daily grind. In the 1978 World Championship he skated magnificently, winning a bronze medal in what was practically a three-way tie for the title. The following year he was second. Everyone acclaimed him as favourite for the Olympic gold.

The media interest and demands on his time became overwhelming. After he had agreed to take part in the Ennia Cup that November, the NSA insisted he give an exhibition at the British ice dance championship – a bait that persuaded television to cover this event for the first time in many years. Cousins found himself literally torn in two. After competing in the short programme section he caught a charter plane from The Hague to the East of England airport to give his exhibition in Nottingham. With very little sleep, he was off the next morning to fly back to Holland to compete in the free skating. He just barely won the event and in his autobiography has strongly criticised the NSA for making him go through that hectic schedule. It is unknown for a skater to leave the site of a competition during an event.

Then came the Olympic year, 1980. In January he won the European title in spite of changing his planned triple jump in the short programme to a double – a decision that resulted in Fassi calling him 'chicken'. Now confirmed as the favourite for the Olympic gold, four and a half million television viewers stayed up till 4 a.m. on a Thursday night to watch live BBC coverage from Lake Placid. It was not his best performance ever but it was sufficient. The only problem came when he went to accept his medal from Lord Killanin. He tripped and nearly went flying.

The favourite to succeed Cousins as Olympic men's champion is his former rinkmate, Scott Hamilton, USA. The pair champions could be any of four pairs, Elena Valova and Oleg Vasiliev from Leningrad, Sabine Baess and Tassilo Thierbach from Karl Marx Stadt in East Germany, Barbara Underhill and Paul Martini from Ontario, and Kitty and Peter Carruthers from Wilmington, Delaware. The women's event is even more open. No woman has stayed at the top for two consecutive seasons since Trixie Schuba won every title in 1971 and 1972 although Linda Fratianne and Anett Poetzsch both won the World title twice. The World champion, Rosalynn Sumners from Seattle, is expected to be strongly challenged by Katarina Witt from Karl Marx Stadt, Claudia Leistner from Mannheim, West Germany, Elaine Zayak from New Jersey, and Elena Vodorezova from Moscow.

Until Elena won a bronze medal in the 1983 World Championship no Russian woman had gained a world championship medal in a singles event. She had to overcome arthritis in the knee to do that and survive the sacking, in spring 1983, of her coach Stanislav Zhuk. However, to get to the top every competitor has had his or her share of seemingly unsurmountable odds. To conquer them has always been part of the joy of becoming a champion.

3

The Uneven Path To Glory

Talent is only one of many requisites a skater must have to win an Olympic gold medal. Each year hundreds of very talented boys and girls fall by the wayside because a well-developed support system is lacking. This includes access to artificial ice and good coaching, parental encouragement and financial backing, plus a determined, even mulish character that will enable the skater to ignore daily frustration and laugh at the incredible odds stacked in favour of failure.

Interestingly enough, many of those who have ascended to the heights of the sport originally took up skating on medical advice – the same spirit of determination that enabled them to overcome childish ill-health and injury has carried them through to the very top. Doctors advised Irina Rodnina's mother that skating might build up stamina in her sickly child. Scott Hamilton, the 1981–3 World champion, afflicted with a rare digestive disease, credits skating with saving his life. As a toddler, an accident with an electric lawnmower sliced off part of Elaine Zayak's foot. Doctors thought skating would encourage her to use both feet equally. In 1982 she became the women's World champion. The 1983 US junior champion, Kathryn Adams, for whom great things are predicted, started skating because the muscles in her legs were weak and uncoordinated. Like all skaters, she has had to overcome injury. In 1980 she broke an elbow. In 1982 she punctured her leg with her blade. The wound required fifteen stitches to close. Later that year she encountered painful back spasms from growing and the impact of landing triple jumps. As a dedicated skater, she sloughs off such setbacks.

Many skaters have demonstrated fierce determination to come back from injury. Robin Cousins won his Olympic gold medal on what he termed second-rate knees after having operations on both of them for torn cartilages. The parents of Dagmar Lurz of West Germany feared she would never walk again after the thirteen-year-old was in a bad car crash. Her coach, Eric Zeller, said she would spend hours a day for months with tears streaming down her face because of the pain, trying to relearn the basic steps of skating. However the metal plate in her hip did not prevent her from winning a bronze medal in the 1980 Winter Olympics.

The enormous surge of interest in skating after John Curry won his Olympic gold medal in 1976, and again after Cousins won in 1980, might have been expected to spark off a growth in the sport at grassroots level. However, because of lack of facilities, this did not occur. Many parts of the country are without rinks at all (Cousins might never have become a skater if a rink had not opened in his home town of Bristol in 1966) and the rinks in existence were soon crowded to capacity. Many, discouraged, did not return after their first, unsatisfactory visit. Others who persevered discovered that the only time they can book lessons on uncrowded ice is either in the morning or late at night since most rinks are run as commercial concerns and have to stay open to the public for recreational skating at convenient times of the day if they are to make money. Parents of primary-level skaters are often unwilling to adjust their lives to this inconvenient schedule, and even though experienced skaters are used to this situation, they still grumble at the abnormal times at which they have to train.

Karen Barber and Nicky Slater, the British second-ranked pair, often appear bleary-eyed during the day because of their marathon after-midnight training sessions at the Richmond rink. They joke that they have jet lag when they take part in competition in Britain because they have to adjust to a different time schedule. Torvill and Dean spend months at the West German Training Centre at Oberstdorf partly because this allows them to practise at more social hours than they could at their home rink in Nottingham. Curry and Cousins both spent their final years as amateurs at the Colorado Ice Arena in Denver. There two ice surfaces permit the demands of the public to be met on one, while the other is kept exclusively for training. There is a second ice surface at the Richmond ice rink but it is extremely small.

First-class coaching is a major factor in producing a champion. If a skater makes a good choice initially, he or she may remain with the same trainer throughout his or her career. Such is the case with the promising

Charles Wildridge, the 1983 British primary champion, executes a Russian split jump. His parents have had to arrange expensive private tutoring to make sure his training does not interfere with his education

American, Brian Boitano, who made his first appearance in the World Championships in 1983, and with the 1983 women's World champion, Rosalynn Sumners. Boitano is taught by Linda Leaver, whom he describes as 'my best friend', and Sumners is coached by Lorraine Borman. Borman said she was astonished at how her job changed once Sumners became US champion in 1982. Overnight her responsibilities blossomed to include protecting her charge from all the excessive intrusions of the media, and she had the unenviable task of deciding which of the flood of invitations Sumners should accept and which exhibitions to turn down. Brian Orser, the Canadian champion, remained with his first trainer, Doug Leigh, in spite of pressure from his national association, once he began to show promise, to leave his home town of Orillia and train in Toronto with one of Canada's leading teachers. The relationship between student and teacher must develop and mature as the skater ages, and Orser said he and Leigh weathered some stormy sessions while he went through a trying adolescence.

Previously unknown internationally, the success of their pupils has brought these coaches worldwide fame so that the parents of potential champions now seek them out and, if they wish, their fortunes can be made. Most skaters change coaches regularly, taking instruction from more and more famous, and more and more expensive, teachers as their careers bloom. Others flit like butterflies from coach to coach as their parents become dissatisfied with the progress their child is making.

If a child demonstrates sufficient talent, a top-level coach may offer to teach him or her on a delayed-payment basis. The bill will become due after the skater signs a substantial contract with an ice show. Dorothy Hamill became a pupil of the Italian-American coach, Carlo Fassi, in 1971. At that time he was teaching Julie Holmes, who was second in the 1971 World Championship and came fourth in the following Olympic Games. When Holmes decided not to enter the 1972 World Championship, Hamill, who was the US team reserve, went in her place. There is always a clear-out of competitors after the World Championship following the Olympics, but Hamill was able to get ahead of the queue of newcomers by establishing her reputation in this event. Her career made steady progress until she won the 1976 Olympic gold medal. When Fassi later brought a court case against Hamill and her parents alleging non-payment of fees, Hamill countersued with a charge of slander. The case was settled with the agreement that neither party talk about the terms. However, Fassi's Italian temperament makes it difficult for him to conceal emotion and he was observed in a jubilant mood the following day.

Bad instructors on the whole tend not to survive long in this results-oriented business but the career of the promising Yugoslav, Sanda Dubravcic, who was second in the 1981 European Championship, was

Kathryn Adams, USA, who has overcome a number of injuries to achieve outstanding success as a junior

Anett Poetzsch of East Germany wipes away a tear after winning the 1980 Olympic gold medal

stunted because the wrapped leg fault in her jumping was not corrected. This occurs when skaters, striving for rotation in jumps, wrap one leg around the other. As a result a landing can be held although the body has not completed the correct number of revolutions. In Dubravcic's case, the fault was too engrained to be eradicated at such a late stage of her career and her world standing has declined as she has aged.

Some instructors may feel their job is confined to teaching and are unwilling to accompany their pupils to competitions since this means a temporary loss of income from their other pupils. (In some cases the loss is permanent as other pupils become jealous of the attention the favoured skater is receiving and seek coaching elsewhere.) However a young competitor is at an enormous handicap without the support of a trainer. When Debbie Cottrill, the British champion in 1978 and 1981, competed in her first international event in Canada a few days after her fifteenth birthday, she lacked the emotional support of a coach, a parent, or a team manager. After the last school figures practice she discovered she had been training on the wrong figures. She had not been informed of a rule change made a few months earlier. Before the free skating her nose started to bleed. An alert coach might have persuaded the referee to let her skate a little later when the bleeding had stopped. Instead, she performed with one nostril blocked with gauze which hindered her breathing, making it hard for her to complete her four-minute routine. It was not surprising she made a less than spectacular showing.

Cottrill was fortunate in living across the road from the Solihull ice rink which opened when she was three. Very many children are introduced too late to the sport for them to compete successfully as singles skaters. The East Germans, who do extremely well in singles and pair skating, have only three skating centres which are used to ensure the maximum amount of competitive success. Five is considered the ideal starting age. A great many children are screened and those accepted into the training programme are expected to show constant progress. The dead wood is vigilantly pruned at all stages so that it is possible, there, to be a seven-year-old failure. This ruthlessness produces youngsters with great potential. The 1980 Olympic champion, Anett Poetzsch, was only twelve, then the minimum age, when she was entered for the 1973 World Championship and was placed a very creditable fourteenth out of twenty-eight. Because Janina Wirth, also from East Germany, won the 1982 World Junior Championship, she was permitted to enter the senior event, even though she was fourteen, a year younger than the current minimum age, and gained twelfth place out of thirty-four.

In Britain there are national competitions for many categories, including boys and girls under eight. The clear winner from dozens of entrants in the 1983 Haig Oundjian under-eight girls contest at the Queens ice rink was Nicola Gregory, a wide-eyed seven-year-old from Sunderland with a short, brunette Dorothy Hamill hairdo, who is also a trampoline expert. The previous year she had won the Richmond under-eights

Nicola Gregory carries off the trophies

Sachelle Barry is a promising under-eights competitor

contest. The winner of this contest in 1983 had much of her glory stolen by Lindsay Jayne Kaszubowski from Bristol who may never become a champion skater but at three and three-quarters proved she already possesses the ability to milk the audience while playing to the judges. She began her one-and-a-half minute routine by skating completely around the rink waving to the audience.

The judges, of course, find such shenanigans impossible to mark. However, the mothers, and some fathers, dutifully take down all the marks and carefully work out their children's relative positions. Most of those taking part in these events are merely fulfilling the frustrated dreams of their parents who stand at the side of the rink shouting encouragement and criticism to their overdressed and overcoiffured progeny. Nevertheless the youngsters sometimes rebel, refuse to skate, and burst into tears. And heaven help the trainer whose pupil did not finish as high as expected. He will be required to explain exactly why.

The pressure that the East Germans put on their promising skaters is as bad as that applied by pushy stage parents in the West. Because the East Germans stress the athletic approach, with much attention paid to triple jumps often at the expense of gracefulness, they suffer a large number of accidents and an early burn-out rate. Their officials try to encourage top-level competitors to carry on, even though they have often expressed the desire to retire. Anett Poetzsch, who underwent a knee cartilage operation after she had regained her World title in 1980, did not wish to continue competing. However, she was entered, and then withdrawn, from the 1981 European Championship. The same thing happened before the World Championship. Finally, a few hours after the East German officials had left the country for Hartford in the United States where the World Championships were to be held, Poetzsch declared publicly that she had retired.

Jan Hoffmann, winner of the 1974 World Championship, was a little more pliant. A knee cartilage operation forced him to sit out the 1975 season but, although he wanted to retire to concentrate on his studies to become a doctor, he was persuaded to remain in the sport. He did not do well in the 1976 Olympic Games, but went on to win a silver medal in 1980. A few weeks later, in the World Championship, he had the satisfaction of beating his Olympic victor, Robin Cousins.

The Russians, having more facilities for youngsters than the East Germans, are not forced to start their training programme so early. When the Protopopovs began skating there was only one indoor rink in the whole of the USSR, then still recovering from the devastation of the Second World War. Today, in their former home town of Leningrad, there is a magnificent three-rink training complex, and skaters are produced as well at centres other than Moscow and Leningrad; the most famous being Sverdlovsk.

Stanislav Zhuk's recent sacking was a milestone in Russian skating history. He was in at the start of the Soviet race for domination in pair skating, producing Rodnina and Ulanov and, when she turned to an easier disciplinarian for guidance, engineering the one-and-a-half pairs (tiny girls matched with fully grown partners) who altered the whole aspect of that event. He then directed the careers of leading singles skaters, including Elena Vodorezova and Alexander Fadeev. His dismissal demonstrates that the Soviets not only have depth in the number of competitors in all four disciplines, but also of coaches. They have reached the stage where they can afford to sweep one of their members under the carpet without worrying about resulting effects. Their country has come a long way in a relatively short time. They won't relinquish this position without a strong fight and if other countries are to gain the top spots, they will have to increase their devotion to training and their efforts to attract youngsters into the sport.

Indoor rinks in the USSR are the exclusive preserve of ice hockey players and competitive figure skaters. In the West it is the recreational skaters, taking part in the activity for pleasure, who pay for the maintenance of the rinks. Recession, and escalating fuel costs, have caused many to close, among them the famous Santa Monica Chalet in California where John Nicks used to teach many top Americans, including the 1979 World pair champions, Tai Babilonia and Randy Gardner.

The East German and USSR systems may have their advantages but, all the same, the freer rein given to Western skaters allows individual talent to break through. Though the Russians have consulted the principal dance choreographers in their country, none has been able to produce a routine such as that shown by John Curry in the 1976 season, or the 'Mack and Mabel' programme with which Torvill and Dean delighted audiences. Curry has said that because he was so familiar with the music

Two talented 11-year-old ice dancers, Natasha Smith and Paul Knepper

he had chosen, Minkus's *Don Quixote* ballet music, and knew exactly what he wanted to do in the programme, it only took him twenty minutes to work out his five minutes of choreography. For Torvill and Dean the task took much longer, sometimes a whole day for just a few seconds' worth of steps. Dean has said the most difficult part was fitting the various parts together so that they flowed smoothly. They were able to devise the intricate moves that fit the music so well because they are masters of their medium, the ice. Most of the Russians' choreography looks exactly what it is – transposed movements from the stage that do not adapt easily onto skates.

John Nicks argues that nothing is more productive of success than a mother making sure her child gets the most out of a £6 twenty-minute lesson by ensuring the child practises each point learned to the maximum of his or her ability. Nevertheless, money problems have caused the downfall of many skaters. Ronnie Robertson, an American who is be-lieved to have spun faster than anyone else, won the silver medal in the 1956 Olympics but had to cut short his competitive career because of lack of funds, to join an ice show when he was only sixteen. Don McPherson of Canada was so short of money that his father was forced to sell his life insurance policy to finance his son's trip to Italy for the 1963 World Championships. McPherson skated outstandingly, to become the youngest-ever men's World champion at the age of sixteen, a record which stands today. He would have liked to remain in competition until the Olympics the following year, but the money just wasn't available. He settled for an ice show contract, and the opportunity to pay back his father.

Nowadays the NSA pays for British skaters' (but not their coaches') travel expenses to international championships. In addition to these are the international competitions which have proliferated since the accept-ance of sponsorship for amateur events in recent years. Such events are generous with their invitations to talented performers who have already proved themselves. One contest organiser, knowing that television coverage would be guaranteed if Cousins agreed to compete, even offered to arrange his travel by Concorde. The NSA also helps promising skaters with their coaching bills. However, the sport is developing at such a rate that more and more time must be invested in it – and that can make it difficult to hold down a normal job. In spite of Sports Aid Foundation help, Torvill and Dean were under enormous pressures until the Nottingham council voted them a grant.

Not all top British skaters are covered by the NSA grant system. For a time even when he was British champion Mark Pepperday received no help from it. Alison Southwood of Sunderland was removed from the scheme after she lost her third position in the British rankings. It could not have happened at a worse time. Her father had been made redundant

Tracey Wainman, Canada, aged 12, after competing in the 1980 World Championship. As she grew her jumping ability declined and she was a case of early burn-out by the time she was 13

Lisa and Neil Cushley execute a forward inside death spiral

and he could only find part-time work. Southwood struggled and determinedly survived but was not put back on the scheme even after she was placed second in the 1982 British Championship. She suffered a stunning blow when the international championship selection committee preferred Susan Jackson, whom she had beaten for the 1983 European and World Championships. When Karen Wood, the British champion, was withdrawn from the World Championship for disciplinary reasons after pulling out of the European Championship at the halfway stage, Southwood was substituted at the last minute. Not surprisingly, she did not do herself justice, so the NSA were able to claim their judgement was correct.

Many youngsters tend to miss a lot of schooling. Lisa and Neil Cushley are a promising couple who compete in both singles and pairs events. When their father went to their school to ask for more time off for the children to compete in the British senior championships, their headmaster mentioned that they were missing a lot of school. Mr Cushley answered that in these troubled economic times the headmaster could not guarantee the children a job, no matter how well they did at school. However, they appear to have a glowing future ahead of them through their skating.

Barbara Graham, technical director of the Canadian Figure Skating Association, says real commitment is demanded from the young skaters who receive their financial help. They are expected to practise from three to four hours a day and their schooling is arranged to accommodate absences for training and competition. As long as they are doing well in competition this is sanctioned by the government. Skaters in the United States and Canada are helped to keep up with their schooling by the excellent government-approved correspondence courses originally intended for children living in remote areas.

Parents must also pay a price for their children's skating success and, too often, this is divorce. Ginny Fratianne got up for years at 3.45 am to chauffeur her daughter, Linda, sometimes driving as much as 100 miles a day shuttling between three ice rinks and a dance studio. When Linda, then sixteen, won the World Championship in 1977 in spite of a viral infection, her father proudly wore a pin declaring he was Father of the Champion. However, the strain on her home life grew. Fratianne said his daughter's coach saw more of Ginny than he did. Divorce was the outcome.

Most families do muddle through, breathing a sigh of relief when their offspring's competitive days are over. When the three-time British champion Yvonne Sugden retired at the advanced age of sixteen in 1956, she explained that part of her problem was that her mother had to accompany her abroad for two months of the year just when her father's career was at its busiest and he needed her support the most. Dorothy Hamill's mother spent five years in a commuter marriage, back and forth between Denver, where her daughter trained, and her husband on the East Coast. To add to her isolation, Fassi, her coach, would not let her into the ice rink when Dorothy was training or when she was competing.

The sacrifice is compounded when the child does not succeed. No one can teach determination, and yet this is a vital part of the make-up of any champion. Trixie Schuba of Austria, who won the World title twice, was said to have all the grace of a camel. Yet she was determined to succeed. As a free skater she was merely adequate, and so she worked on her school figures with such an intensity that her technique was acclaimed as far beyond that of her rivals. Her mind was completely oblivious to anything but her slowly traced circles. Having built her lead in this initial section, she controlled her nerves to give the best free-skating performance she could and won the 1972 Olympic gold medal. Skating to 'The Impossible Dream' from *Man of La Mancha* she achieved what for many *was* impossible. Very few people would have bet on her success, but she herself never wavered from the belief that she could do it.

Far right: John Curry seen in a pivot move in 1975, the year before he won all the international championships

Right: Linda Fratianne demonstrating an outside spread. Her coach insisted she worked with someone in the entertainment world to learn how to relate to audiences

4

The Singles Competition

The best exponents of singles skating – people like Peggy Fleming, John Curry and Robin Cousins – transcend the strict athletic and competitive requirements of the sport, adding an elegance to its basic moves that raises skating to the level of an art form to be appreciated by even the most inexpert of spectators. Their allocated time on the ice flashes by, leaving audiences cheering for more. Less talented skaters can be almost as enjoyable to watch, if the spectator understands a little more of what the skater is trying to achieve.

Singles competitions consist of three sections: the school figures, worth 30 per cent of the overall event; the short programme, worth 20 per cent; and the free skating, worth 50 per cent. It is the last portion, with its exciting spins and jumps executed to stirring music, that is most often shown on television.

Free Skating
Women at senior level are required to skate for four minutes and men for four-and-a-half in their free-skating programme. Both are allowed ten seconds leeway either way. If the electronic timing device shows less than 3:50 or 4:20 from the moment the skater started to move, the referee instructs the panel of judges to deduct accordingly from the marks. If it shows over 4:10 or 4:40, the referee immediately blows a whistle and the judges stop watching.

The skater may present whatever he or she likes in the free programme, with some exceptions, such as the somersault. This movement, previously confined to professional ice shows, was introduced to amateur skating by Terry Kubicka, USA, in the 1976 Olympic Games but the ISU soon decided it was too flashy for competitive purposes. Perhaps they were influenced by Kubicka's unfortunate accident in the bubble practice rink in Innsbruck when he slashed his blade through the thin ice surface into one of the plastic pipes containing freezing material, thereby putting the rink out of action for twenty-four hours. Kubicka did his somersault with his knees tucked into his body. Television viewers may be familiar with the more difficult version executed professionally by Robin Cousins, in which his legs are kept straight out.

Certain moves are included by all the top exponents. The most common is the double axel jump, when the skater takes off forward on an outside edge and lands backwards on the outside edge of the other foot after rotating two-and-a-half times in the air. Since axels are almost the only jumps with a forward take-off, they are relatively easy to spot. However, to recognise other jumps the spectator needs to become familiar with edges, a term that is often heard in television commentaries but may not always be understood.

The bottom of a skating blade is not flat, but hollow ground with a concave middle part. When the skater stands upright both edges rest on the ice, but when he leans to the right one edge leaves the ice so that he is balanced on the outside edge on the right foot and the inside edge on the left. When he leans to the left he rests on the left outside edge and the right inside edge.

Parts of a skate

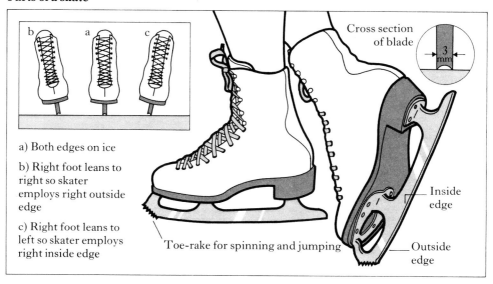

a) Both edges on ice

b) Right foot leans to right so skater employs right outside edge

c) Right foot leans to left so skater employs right inside edge

Cross section of blade

Inside edge

Outside edge

Toe-rake for spinning and jumping

The very first jump that any skater learns, the three jump, uses the same take-off and landing edges as the axel. The skater takes off from the outside edge of one foot, going forwards, and lands backwards on the other foot on an outside edge, having turned 180°. The axel involves turning one-and-a-half times in the air, through 540°. It was first introduced by the Norwegian, Axel Paulsen, in the nineteenth century, but he did a very primitive version of the beautiful, soaring move seen today. At the zenith of her competitive career the highlight of Sonja Henie's routine was two axels in a row. She would wind herself up like a corkscrew, signalling that the move was to come. This is now deemed bad form. She did not get very far off the ice, either. Today, skaters jump so high that the rotation is relatively easy. The height of Robin Cousins's jumps never fails to draw gasps of admiration, particularly the tuck and delayed axels. In the tuck axel the legs are brought up to the body, accentuating the skater's height above the ice. In the delayed axel the rotation is held off until the last moment.

Dick Button, the 1948 and 1952 Olympic gold-medal winner who brought in the flying camel and was the first person to accomplish a triple jump, was responsible for introducing the double axel. To accomplish this, the skater turns two-and-a-half times, or 900°, in the air. Peggy Fleming produced a further refinement, a move few others have been able to repeat. Her speciality was to take off for a double axel from an outside spreadeagle position (both feet on the ice, one pointing forwards and the other backwards) and immediately resume it on landing. However, when she won the gold medal in the 1968 Olympic Games in Grenoble she reduced the difficulty of this move, choosing to execute a single rather than a double axel.

The first person to do a triple axel in a World Championship was Vern Taylor of Canada, in 1978. Brian Orser, also a Canadian, presented a much smoother version of the jump with its three-and-a-half turns – that's 1260° – in his first appearance in a World Championship in 1981. The following year he was still the only competitor to execute this move and became known as Mr Triple Axel. However – so quickly do technical

Triple axel

barriers fall these days – in 1983 four other skaters also accomplished this jump in the World Championship. Indeed, the Russian champion, Alexander Fadeev, went one step further, combining his triple axel with a double toe loop jump. He also did a double axel landing in a back sit spin and tried, unsuccessfully, a quadruple toe loop. No one has yet accomplished a quad in competition but Fadeev, Orser, and two Americans, Brian Boitano and Mark Cockerell, have executed them in practice. This barrier will, no doubt, fall soon.

Skating blades have teeth at the front called toe rakes or picks. These are used in certain jumps almost as a pole vaulter uses his pole. Because of this, competitors in the free skating use skates with very big bottom toes. The toe loop is the simplest of the one-rotation (360°) jumps. The skater takes off on a right back outside edge, digging his left toe rake into the ice to assist the take-off, and turns counter-clockwise for a full revolution before landing on his right leg on a back outside edge.

In 1980 Grzegorz Filipowski, the 13-year-old Polish champion, made history by combining two triple jumps, both toe loops, in the World Championship. His marks did not reflect this accomplishment and he was placed thirteenth out of twenty-two in this section. The West German press complained that he was given marks for his height, not for his skating ability, and the organisers presented him with the trophy for

Double toe loop

the unluckiest skater. Since then Cockerell has performed the combination, while Fadeev has combined two different triple jumps, the salchow and the toe loop.

Double and triple toe loops are a very familiar part of all competitions and are sometimes known by other names. Some Britons call toe loops cherry flips, or talk about a 'cherry'. Americans confuse the issue further by calling a certain version of toe loop – in which a left one-foot turn is made before stepping onto the take-off foot – a toe walley.

Almost all jumps are landed on a back outside edge since this is the most stable position for landing. Just as people can be right or left-handed, skaters can be right or left-footed. Most skaters choose to land on their right foot but a minority, like the 1981 and 1983 World champions, Denise Biellmann of Switzerland, and Rosalynn Sumners, USA, opt for their left. This means all their jumps will be mirror images of the illustrations in this book. (Interestingly a right-handed person is not necessarily right-footed.)

No routine is complete without a double or triple lutz. In this jump the skater goes backwards on his left outside edge, generally for long enough to alert the spectator that the lutz is coming. Sometimes he will even glance nervously over his shoulder to check on his progress. He then digs his right toe into the ice, but instead of rotating in the natural direction (which would be clockwise) he goes against the normal flow of his body and rotates counter-clockwise. This makes the jump very difficult. The skater lands on a right back outside edge having done one, two or three complete revolutions in the air.

Additionally, since the approach to this jump is against the normal pattern of movement on a public rink, the jump is very difficult to practise. The skater has to check continually that he is not about to collide with someone. John Curry partly attributed his low double lutz to the crowded conditions of the Richmond rink where he trained for several years. Susan Jackson, an improving top-level British skater who changed, in 1983, from her home rink in Nottingham to Richmond to obtain the best school-figures instruction from Arnold Gerschwiler, also found the crowded conditions a problem.

Single lutz

The triple lutz was first accomplished in a World Championship by Donald Jackson of Canada in 1962. His performance was enough to gain the title and the most number of sixes ever given in that event – a record he retained until Torvill and Dean took over that particular niche in history in 1982. Well behind in the school figures, which then accounted for 60 per cent of the event, his free skating, which included other innovations such as jumping with his arms above his head or with his arms folded, was so electrifying that the first to congratulate him was the mother of his rival, Karol Divin, who, skating in his home town, Prague, had held the lead until then.

Jackson later revealed that he had landed the triple lutz only four times before. He attempted the move because he was feeling so good that day. The triple lutz was not accomplished again in international championships until Jan Hoffmann of East Germany won the European and World titles twelve years later. Although Robin Cousins did triple lutzes in practice and used them to disconcert Vladimir Kovalev, USSR, one of his main opponents in the 1980 European Championship, he did not find it necessary to include this jump in his competitive routines. Commentating for BBC television during the 1983 World Championships, Cousins expressed his amazement that more than half the men in that event successfully presented the triple lutz in combination with a double toe loop in the short programme division. It was yet another mark of skating's technical progress.

Denise Biellmann was the first woman to do a triple lutz, landing this jump in the 1978 European Championship and so impressing the British judge, Pauline Borrajo, that she awarded her a six for technical merit. Although sixes are often given for artistic impression, this was believed to be the first awarded for technical merit to a woman in modern times. Biellmann was not able to repeat the jump until she won the World title in 1981. In 1983 two women attempted the move, Kay Thomson of

Alexander Fadeev demonstrates the perfect landing position, with shoulders locked at right angles to the skate's backward progression

In 1983 Scott Hamilton decided to forgo the sparkles and sequins that normally adorn skating outfits in an effort to give skating a more masculine image

Double flip

Canada and Agnes Grosselin of France. The jump appears to present an insurmountable barrier for most women competitors.

Quite often, in error, the skater changes from a back outside edge to a back inside edge before putting his toe rake in the ice for the take-off. This turns the move into another jump called a flip rather than a lutz. Although single and double flips are common, a triple flip is considered extremely hard to execute. Katarina Witt of East Germany, the 1983 European champion, became the first woman to do this move and stay upright. That was accomplished in the 1983 World Championship, but it was not enough to rescue her from her poor school-figures placing and she did not gain a place on the podium. Very few men have executed the triple flip in a World Championship. Even the 1983 title holder, Scott Hamilton, USA, who had been planning to demonstrate this jump, changed his mind in the air and did the easier double instead. The omission was not enough to cost him his title, however.

The flip is occasionally called a toe salchow since it is a salchow jump in which the toe is used. Named after the Swede, Ulrich Salchow, who won many World titles at the beginning of the century, the salchow is a jump from the back inside edge of the left foot, rotating in a counter-clockwise direction, and landing on the back outside edge of the right

Triple salchow

Alexander Fadeev about to take off in a triple salchow. He is tipped for high honours in 1985, when many top contenders will have left the amateur scene after Olympic year

Scott Hamilton showing the muscular pull needed to achieve triple rotation in a jump

foot after one, two or three full rotations. The jump is pronounced sal-cow, and skaters often shorten the name to 'sal' as in 'Have you seen my double sal?' Cecilia Colledge was the first woman to do a double jump, which was a salchow. The first woman to do a triple jump in a World Championship was Sonja Morgenstern of East Germany in 1971, and she also chose a salchow.

When Dick Button decided to work on the first triple jump he chose the loop though it is now considered much harder than the triple toe loop or the triple salchow. He did so because he had a very strong double loop and could jump three double loops in combination. The loop jump is easily recognised because it is, as its name suggests, a simple loop in the air. The same foot and edge are used in the take-off and landing, right back outside to right back outside rotating counter-clockwise.

Triple loop

To watch some of the men's routines up until the 1984 season, it might have been thought free skating consisted of nothing more than jumping. One competitor in the 1983 World Championship, for example, presented only one item that was not a jump in his entire $4\frac{1}{2}$-minute routine – an extremely short spin. The ISU countered this trend in June 1983 by issuing very precise regulations for the free skating, similar to those in use for the pair events, which laid down certain minimums and severely curtailed the number of repetitions permitted.

Both men and women in senior competition must now do four spins, one of which must contain a combination of positions. The men must do two sets of footwork, either straight line, circular or serpentine, which fully utilise the ice surface. The women must do one set of footwork and one set of spirals (gliding arabesques) and spreadeagles. Skaters may not repeat the same type of triple jump, although one may be repeated if it is combined with another jump.

These regulations will particularly handicap skaters such as Elaine Zayak, USA, who are known for their jumping ability. Zayak won the 1982 World Championship, stunning the audience with six triple jumps, four of which were toe loops (two of those in combination with other jumps), and two triple salchows. Her showing was enough to catapult her from seventh place at the halfway stage to win. Now, however, she will be limited to only one triple toe loop and one triple salchow, one of which may be repeated in combination with another jump.

Spectators at the professional ice shows tend to applaud spins but largely ignore jumps, unless they are performed by someone like Cousins, whose jumps are so spectacularly high. Yet spins have not developed much in the past few decades. Ronnie Robertson, who won the Olympic silver medal in 1956, is believed to have been the fastest spinner ever. His arms would pull so strongly against the centrifugal force that specks of blood would ooze through his pores. Skaters have to learn to ignore giddiness. Robertson learnt so well that when NASA tested him in their antigravity chamber, they could not even make him dizzy.

Spins can be done in almost any position. Cousins performed a variation of the sit spin in which he pulled his head down into his lap, and this was copied by other skaters. Cousins, John Curry and Toller Cranston of Canada were all known for their excellent arabesque positions on their camel spins, so called because novice skaters cannot bring their leg high enough to form an arabesque and their position is marred by a hump. A popular way of completing a routine is with a basic stand spin. Scott Hamilton uses this move extremely effectively. His blurring image is guaranteed to bring an audience to its feet.

Spinning is done on the primary foot on a back inside edge, or on the flat of the blade with its weight towards the front. (In an unusual case, such as Cousins's and Cranston's camel spins, a forward outside edge is employed. This aids the line of the spin but is extremely advanced.) Most skaters spin on their left foot counter-clockwise. Advanced skaters change feet while spinning. On their second foot they rotate in the same direction as before, but on a back outside edge which is more difficult.

When John Curry went to the United States to train he worked briefly with Gus Lussi, the coach who had guided Dick Button towards the world's first triple jump. Curry was having problems with his triple

Norbert Schramm executes a butterfly jump

Denise Biellmann demonstrates 'her' spin

Middle: Robin Cousins, practising at the 1978 World Championship, demonstrates a good arabesque position

Bottom: Toller Cranston of Canada, one of the sport's most entertaining characters, performs his famous Russian split

jumps. Lussi immediately decided Curry spun on the wrong foot, and insisted he try to spin the other way round. It was pretty humiliating having to go through all the basic moves again – dancers learn everything on both feet in both directions, but skaters are one-direction people. However, Lussi's advice paid off. Learning to spin in the same direction in which he rotated his jumps in the air helped Curry to speed his airborne revolutions. A by-product was that he was able to introduce a spin first one way and then the other, an unusual choreographic feature, into his breathtaking Olympic programme.

The layback, one of the most attractive spins to watch, was used by Peggy Fleming to great advantage. Denise Biellmann has a variation which delights everyone who sees it. She grabs her foot and hoists it above her head so that it obscures her view of the stadium ceiling. She pays a high price for her gymnastic ability, however. When she leaves the ice after doing her spin she has to lie down for half an hour with ice packs on her back.

The top-level skater combines spins and jumps. Nearly every routine contains a flying camel – in which the skater jumps from one foot to the other, briefly taking a position in the air which, when done well, resembles a butterfly – to land in an arabesque position and execute a back camel spin. The skater can also land in a back sit spin, in which case the move is known as a death drop. It takes a lot of nerve to execute this move and much practice time is spent wiping ice flakes from the skater's backside. Although protective wear is available, skaters almost never use cushioning. Cousins's mother had to use a combination of threats and persuasion to make him wear rubber padding after he had incurred some particularly bad bruises while learning an advanced jump.

In one way skating is easy to judge. If one skater seems to be enjoying his routine and the four-and-a-half minutes flash by, the programme is a success. If another is labouring so that every move appears to involve great effort and time drags, the routine is bad. The two skaters may be technically matched, but the first will win both the judges' marks and the audience's applause. The enjoyment factor is a definite consideration.

The two categories for which free skating is marked, technical merit and artistic impression, are equally important, except when a judge gives the same total marks. In this case the first mark, for technical merit, is used to break the tie. In theory it is possible for a skater who presents a programme lacking in difficulty to receive high marks in the second category. In practice, unfortunately, the judges rarely vary the free skating marks by more than three-tenths of a point. This has encouraged skaters to strive for technical achievement at the expense of style, and to include jumps they haven't fully mastered.

Polished performances, such as John Curry gave in 1976, are all too rare. Often skaters' ideas of artistry are limited to waving their arms around haphazardly. Curry, who had late but lengthy ballet training, used both inside and outside spreadeagles to great effect. His dance expertise gave him the hip turnout needed for these moves. It also nearly cost him the 1976 European Championship gold medal since he included alternate inside and outside spreadeagles as a method of getting gracefully from one end of the rink to the other during his short programme routine. The Russians, having watched him in practice, decided this was an illegal extra move and began lobbying the judges to point it out. Fortunately Curry's trainer, Carlo Fassi, was well respected by the judges and one of their number explained what was happening. The spreadeagles immediately disappeared from his routine.

By contrast, Robin Cousins adopted disco steps into his routines, and would insert snazzy, jazzy footwork which often ended with a high-kick. In this way he came to grief in the 1980 World Championship in Dortmund. The intricate footwork of his short programme was never a problem until that last competitive appearance when a second's inattention became a moment's sitting on the ice. Cousins would also highlight his programme with Russian split jumps. No one, however, could match Toller Cranston in these. A bronze medal winner in the 1976 Olympic Games, he achieved a wonderful position in the air with his legs stretched out in a straight line and his fingers clasping at the tips of his boots.

The 'right' choice of music matters, too. Images of John Curry are immediately conjured up by skating fans when they hear Minkus's *Don Quixote* ballet music; they groan when other skaters misuse this. In 1974 Dorothy Hamill abandoned *Finlandia* and the music from *Limelight* which she had been practising to for six months to return to a previous selection. Although she was performing well to the new music, she felt the routine lacked that indefinable factor that moves audiences. The NSA asked Cousins to bring back the music from the film of *The Railway Children*, which he had used for his short programme so effectively during one season. Cousins had tired of this piece, but he recognised that it had a quality which complimented his skating, and so he complied.

Short programme

This section is worth 20 per cent of the event and was introduced in the 1972–3 season. Skaters were then required to perform six elements – now extended to seven. Those selected for the 1984 Olympic season were:

1. Double flip jump

2. Double axel jump

3. A two-jump combination with either the first or second jump a double loop. This can be combined with the same jump or any other double or triple jump

Terry Kubicka, USA, demonstrates a back flip of the kind he did in the 1976 Olympics, subsequently outlawed by the ISU

John Curry's balletically inspired outfits antagonised the skating fraternity

4. A death drop in which there must be at least six rotations in the back sit spin

5. A change foot camel spin with at least five revolutions on each foot

6. A spin with a combination of positions and a change of foot

7. A straight-line step sequence.

These may be performed in any order to music of the skater's choice. There is no minimum time limit but the seven elements must be completed in two minutes. Skaters who make a mistake in one of the elements are not allowed to try the move again. This puts great pressure on the top competitors. In the 1973 World Championship Janet Lynn buckled under the pressure and made major errors on three elements. She was placed twelfth in this section, a generous assessment, and finished second overall in what was her last amateur competitive appearance.

Two marks are given for the short programme. The first is for the required elements, with specific deductions for mistakes. The second is for presentation. Unlike the free skating, there is often a wide disparity between the two marks. A high second mark is frequently used to keep the favourite in contention even when that skater has performed badly.

School figures

A skating blade is curved from front to back. This curvature is called a radius and it is because of this, and because the blade has two edges, that figure skating is possible. All school figures are variations on the basic figure eight in which the skater does a circle on one foot, returning to the point at which he set out, and then does a circle on the other foot, ending up by having drawn an eight on the ice. The blade actually causes the ice under it to melt because of the pressure it exerts. As soon as it has passed the ice refreezes, but a track or tracing remains. If the skater is not on one edge, but on the flat of the blade, two parallel lines will appear on the ice. This is one of the worst faults in figure skating. The other main fault is to put the free foot down except when specifically striking onto the other foot. This incurs a penalty of 1.0 out of the maximum of 6.0.

Top-level skaters almost never make this mistake so there was a gasp of amazement when the defending American World champion, Charlie Tickner, did so in the loop figure in the 1979 World Championship. He ended up fourth, mainly because of that. Alexander Fadeev, USSR, did the same in the rocker figure in the 1983 European Championship.

The circles are expected to have a diameter of three times the skater's height. The bigger a figure is the more it is appreciated by the judges. Vladimir Kovalev, USSR, the 1977 and 1979 World champion, executed huge figures. In spite of Cousins's six-foot stance, his figures were very small, a factor which counted against him. Loop figures are a third of the size of the other school figure but again bigness is desirable.

Figures are rarely shown on television because they are boring to watch. There is no music, and the skaters carry out these exercises extremely slowly. One mark is given by each judge for each of the three figures. The rule-books state that this should reflect the style and posture of the skater as well as the figure's geometry. Today style is completely overlooked, however. Skaters adopt ugly positions striving to get the second tracing position within a millimetre of the first. The judges closely examine the tracings, even getting down on their hands and knees to peer at the lines. It is a trend that many, including John Curry, abhor.

The ISU recognises forty-one figures which are each given a number. In the more advanced figures the skater executes a circle and then, instead of striking off on the other foot, merely changes edge and continues on the same foot for another circle. These are called paragraph figures, and because they take so long to perform, it was recently decided that only two tracings would be required in these figures, rather than the three tracings on each foot that are required in the others. Turns of 180° involving only one foot are included in most figures. These are three turns, bracket turns, rocker turns and counter turns.

The three turn, so called because the tracing left on the ice looks like the number three, is from one edge to another – that is, either outside to inside or inside to outside and from one direction to the other, either forward to backward, or backward to forward, turning in the body's natural flow of movement.

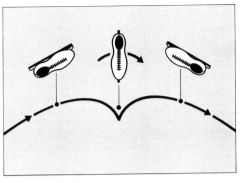

Three turn

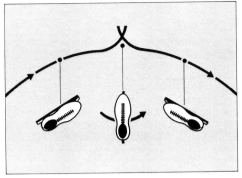

Bracket turn

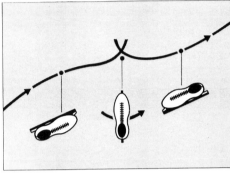

Counter turn

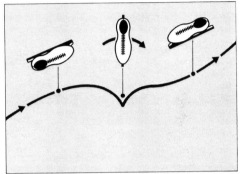

Rocker turn

The bracket turn, which leaves an impression on the ice which looks like a bracket, is also from one edge to the other and one direction to the other, but this time the turning is done against the natural flow of the body which makes this a more difficult turn.

The rocker turn is from one direction to the other but from one edge to the same edge, while turning in the natural flow. The counter turn is from one direction to the other and from one edge to the same edge, but turning against the natural flow of the body.

In addition are the loop figures, which are circles within circles.

Although the quality of figures has improved in recent years because the science of skate-making has developed and ice conditions are much better, judges these days rarely award more than 4.0 marks, even to a World champion. The reason for this is open to speculation, but it could be that the judges know they cannot fool anyone into believing that they used to free skate better than today's performers. However, by keeping the school figures marks down so low they maybe hope to give the impression their figures were better!

An initial deficit in the school figures used to be very hard to overcome. In the 1976 World Championship Toller Cranston of Canada was fifth at the end of this section. He won the short programme, and was second in the free skating, yet he finished only fourth overall. Vladimir Kovalev, USSR, who won the figures, was fifth in the short programme, fourth in the free, and finished second. That result was obviously unfair. Cranston, a flamboyant character, amid much publicity charged to a pool of unfrozen water in Göteborg and threw in his figure skates, at the same time announcing that figures were useless; he would do better to employ his talents elsewhere. In July 1980 a new method of working out the results, without bringing marks forward from each section, was introduced. This system, had it been in effect for the 1976 World Championship, would have given Cranston the silver medal behind John Curry and despatched Kovalev to fourth place (see pages 123–132).

Cranston was not alone in disliking figures. John Curry said he found a couple of hours of figure practice a very civilised way to start the day, providing that was not, as when he trained in England, at the crack of dawn. Robin Cousins was one who merely tolerated figures. In Dortmund in 1980 he could hardly wait till the third figure was over to discard his figure skates and declare he would never do figures again.

The personality of a good figure skater differs a great deal from that of the good free skater. To do good figures you need to be an introvert. You must be able to shut out completely all distractions and concentrate on what you are doing, focusing your attention on that small piece of ice. A good free skater likes to interact with the audience. Norbert Schramm, the 1982 and 1983 European champion, and runner-up for the World title, finds he cannot perform his best without a good-sized audience. Their response as he pulls faces at them eggs him on to skate much better.

It was often believed that Robin Cousins was pushed in the figures – that is, given better marks than he deserved so that such a superlative free skater should be kept within reach of the medals. On one occasion, in the 1979 European Championship, he did a very poor second figure, the left back paragraph brackets. However, one judge still gave him second place in this figure and another placed him third. The British judge, Sally Stapleford, refusing to compromise, gave him the lowest mark he received, a 2.9. Cousins later said it was what he deserved.

Since the spectator cannot go onto the ice to examine the tracings, it is impossible for him to get an accurate impression of the execution of a figure. This means that judges are less subject to overt criticism. Nevertheless Frank Carroll, coach of Linda Fratianne who won the silver medal in the 1980 Olympic Games, said that his pupil was denied the gold because the German-speaking judges acted in collusion, marking up the East and West German competitors in the school figures. (Anett Poetzsch of East Germany won the gold medal and Dagmar Lurz of West Germany the bronze.) There is no way this can be proved or disproved. However, what it does indicate is that there is a very good argument for abolishing school figures in competition.

5

Pair Skating

Pair skating can be the most spectacular of the four disciplines. It is certainly the most dangerous. Done well, it can be breathtakingly beautiful. The Americans, Tai Babilonia and Randy Gardner, were sheer perfection when they won the World title in 1979. Many, too, will recall the artistry and grace of the Protopopovs' gold medal-winning performance in the 1964 and 1968 Olympic Games.

Oleg Protopopov was a survivor of the siege of Leningrad. He met Ludmila Belousova, his future wife, at the first artificial ice rink in the USSR. Officials said they were too old to skate competively, and theirs was an uphill path. Protopopov felt that the love between them enhanced their skating and deplored the existence of the many brother and sister pairs which were very common in the West, since instructors find it far easier to deal with only one set of parents.

The Protopopovs from Leningrad were dethroned in 1969 by Irina Rodnina and Alexei Ulanov of Moscow, who dazzled the judges with their speed, combination of jumps never previously seen in pair skating, and novel lifts. First with Ulanov, and then with Alexander Zaitsev, later to become her husband, Rodnina dominated the sport for over a decade and, in so doing, nearly killed it. Other skaters saw the futility of trying to

Tai Babilonia and Randy Gardner execute a star lift in the 1976 Olympic Games

Elegance on ice – the Protopopovs shortly after winning their second Olympic gold medal

beat the Russians, and retired from amateur competition or turned professional earlier than they might otherwise have done. Eventually even the public tired of the sameness of the event.

In 1977 an even harsher blow was dealt to the sport. The Moscow school took to sending to the international championships one-and-a-half pairs, created by matching girls barely meeting the minimum age requirements – then 12, now 15 – with fully grown, mature partners able to manipulate them like puppets on a string. In their first international season Marina Cherkasova, 12, and Sergei Shakhrai, 18, won bronze medals in the 1977 European Championship and were placed fourth a few weeks later in the World Championship. The success of this couple led other countries to follow the Russians' example. The men began tossing their diminutive partners over the ice as if they were juggling with beach balls.

Cherkasova and Shakhrai's party piece was the quadruple twist lift. When she matured they were not able to repeat the move. Although they won the 1980 World title, it was an uninspiring victory. The following year they failed to win a medal in the World Championship, partly because Shakhrai could not adjust to Cherkasova's new height and weight. Soon afterwards their partnership dissolved.

During this unhappy period, Babilonia and Gardner of the USA were doing their best to bring pair skating back on to a path where the emphasis was on artistry. Their trainer, John Nicks, realising that their style alone was not enough to win the World title, sent them briefly to another coach, Ron Ludington, to increase their repertoire of tricks. The highlight of Babilonia and Gardner's performance was their throw double axel. From a left forward outside edge he would throw her across the rink and she would turn two and a half times, landing on a right back outside edge. Ludington helped them add an even more spectacular throw triple salchow. Babilonia would be thrown from a left backward inside edge and land, after turning three complete revolutions, on a right back outside edge many feet away from her partner.

Rodnina never did throw moves. Her second coach, Tatiana Tarasova, said that it was inelegant for the man to throw away his partner. In fact, she never tried the moves because of fear of injury. Almost all couples suffer knee injuries from throw moves, caused not so much by the impact of landing from such a height but by wrenching the knee on an incorrect landing. Rodnina and Zaitsev fully made up for this absence, however, with moves such as the reverse leg overhead lift.

Zaitsev spent part of his daily training lugging weights around the ice to increase his already significant strength. He was aided in performance by Rodnina's diminutive size – 4 feet 11 inches to his 5 feet 10 inches. Because they were the same size, Babilonia and Gardner could not do twist lifts well, and only accomplished a double twist in their final season. Except for their lovely star and table top lifts they could not match the Russian pair's expertise in and variety of lifts.

When Babilonia and Gardner won their World title in 1979 it was in the absence of Rodnina and Zaitsev; she was having a baby. The top East German pair, Manuela Mager and Uwe Bewersdorf, were missing too, because he was injured. In 1978 the Americans had been third in the World Championship, some distance behind these pairs. The opportunity to see if the Americans could overcome both couples in the 1980 Olympic Games at Lake Placid was lost when Gardner reinjured a groin muscle in the warm-up for the short programme. Rodnina later said she felt that the overwhelming interest of the media had put the Americans under enormous strain, and that the injury partly resulted from it.

This proved to be Rodnina's last contest. She retired having won ten consecutive World titles and gold medals in three Olympic Games, equalling Sonja Henie's record. She also won eleven European titles. Babilonia and Gardner had been hoping that his injury would improve enough for them to compete against the Russians a few weeks later in the World Championship in Dortmund. When the Americans decided this was not possible, Rodnina and Zaitsev were withdrawn – it is believed greatly against Zaitsev's wishes – although they had already arrived in Dortmund, enabling Cherkasova and Shakhrai, silver medallists in Lake Placid, to claim the title by beating the East Germans again. Babilonia

Irina Rodnina and Alexander Zaitsev show perfect form in a one-handed lasso lift in practice at the 1975 World Championship

Rodnina and Zaitsev in a triple twist lift. It was while they were practising this move that other skaters reported seeing slash marks from Rodnina's skates on Zaitsev's chest

and Gardner immediately turned professional at the tender ages of nineteen and twenty-one. Rodnina and Zaitsev were thirty and twenty-seven – an example of how much longer Eastern European skaters remain in competitive skating, free from the pressure to support themselves as amateurs.

Rodnina and Zaitsev had omitted a death spiral from their free skating for the 1980 Olympic Games although they could do all three versions of this move – back outside, back inside and forward inside – extremely well. This is a basic move in pair skating and the ISU consequently brought in stringent regulations specifying that two death spirals must be presented in the free skating. (Later the number was reduced to one, to be of a different kind from the version required in that season's short programme section.) They also detailed the maximum number of times certain types of moves may be tried. They stressed the importance of connecting steps and choreography and reduced the time allowed for the free skating by thirty seconds to four and a half minutes.

With the exception of couples like Babilonia and Gardner, by 1980 pair skating had degenerated into a speed contest in which one-and-a-half pairs concentrated on an endless stream of not very well accomplished throw moves and twist lifts. Pairs with equally-sized partners could only attempt such moves with a very real risk of injury, and as a result more and more dropped out. In 1981 only six pairs competed in the European Championship, the least number since 1950, and eleven in the World Championship, the least since 1959. However, the new regulations with their stress on artistry to make up for a deficit of technical tricks has encouraged new pairs to enter the sport. By 1983 the numbers entering these events had increased to twelve and seventeen.

Short programme

Pair skating used to consist of free skating only. This became increasingly hard to judge and in the mid 1960s the ISU tried an experimental system by which the skaters were required to perform twice, once to familiarise the judges with their routines, and again the following evening to be marked. The judges were soon in a quandary over how to mark those who had done well on the 'preview' evening but went to pieces the second time. The skaters did not like the system, which they found tiring, and shortly afterwards the short programme was introduced. At first the pairs were required to do six elements, with a maximum time limit of two minutes. For the 1982 season a seventh element was added and the maximum time increased by fifteen seconds.

The elements are specified well in advance and are the same for every senior competition that season. They may be done in any order to music of the skaters' choice. The short programme pair elements selected for the 1983–4 season were:

1. Double loop solo jump

2. Double lasso lift

3. Double twist lift

4. Backward outside death spiral

5. Solo change foot sit spins

6. Pair spin

7. Serpentine footwork

The first of these elements, the double loop solo jump, has been described on page 72 and is executed in unison, either as shadow jumps or, if the skaters jump in reverse directions, as mirror images.

In the double lasso lift the man swings his partner over his head, like a lasso. The pair skate forward side by side with the woman's left hand in the man's left hand at hip height and the woman's right hand in his right hand above her head. She takes off on a forward left outside edge. It is a fault if she moves in front of her partner before the take-off. She then swings one complete turn around her partner while getting into the overhead position where they lock their arms straight. They then rotate two full revolutions and he begins to bring her down. She lands, after making a further half turn, on a right back outside edge. The quality of this move is determined by the accuracy of the take-off, the ease with which the woman attains the overhead position, the degree of the split position of her legs in the air, their straightness, the arch of her back, the speed with which the man travels while he is turning and the distance he covers. It is not just a test of the man's skating ability. To get into the overhead position the woman must be able to support and balance her own weight.

In the double twist lift the man aids the woman to get aloft as she takes off from a lutz take-off (see page 69). She turns two complete revolutions and is caught by the man who lowers her onto the ice where she skates off on a right back outside edge.

The death spiral is a classic move in pair skating. It was first done at the beginning of the century by the show skater, Charlotte. However in its present form it was first executed by the Canadians, Suzanne Morrow and Wally Distelmeyer, in 1948. It is so called because the woman's head is so near the ice that the move appears much more dangerous than it in fact is. When things go wrong the man tends to pull the woman right off the ice and she ends up sitting on her bottom. That was where Cynthia Kauffman finished up when her brother made an error in the 1968 Olympic Games – a slip that cost the American champions the bronze medals.

Pair Skating 85

For the change foot sit spins the skaters must do five revolutions on each foot. Often you can hear one partner shout to the other when it's time for them to change feet. In general, men are poorer spinners than women and this will show up in a lack of unison.

In the pair spin the skaters hold onto each other while spinning. They must do at least two changes of position. Most will probably incorporate camel and sit positions. This element had not been in the required moves in previous seasons, and before the start of the 1983–4 season skaters were enjoying themselves experimenting with it.

The footwork sequence has to cover the whole rink making three distinct curves. Though the skaters do not have to hold on to each other, they must have perfect unison.

Like the singles, the short programme is marked in two categories, the first for required elements and the second for presentation. Specific amounts for faults must be deducted from the first mark. It is not always easy for judges to do exactly as they are directed. In the 1981 World Championship the Canadians, Barbara Underhill and Paul Martini, fell so badly while building up speed for their lift that they were unable to get back together to complete it. As the pairs had to accomplish only six elements it seems strange that an experienced judge could miss one of them. Yet this did happen; and even though the judge concerned may have realised her mistake as soon as the other judges' marks were announced, there is no provision for the changing of marks once given.

Free skating

The ISU recently specified that the free skating must contain:

1. Three overhead lifts each of a different nature. One of these may be a twist lift, but there may not be more than two kinds of twist lifts

2. Two solo jumps done in unison

3. One sequence of jump combinations; the skaters may choose the number of jumps

4. One pair spin in which a combination of positions must be used

5. One solo spin done in unison

6. One death spiral other than that season's prescribed short programme death spiral

7. One set of footwork

8. One sequence of one or more spirals and/or such free skating moves as turns, pivots, and temporary separations of the partners

9. An optional throw lift

This is the minimum that pair skaters must present in their four-and-a-half minute routine, and specific points are deducted if they fail to provide any of the elements named above. They are allowed to present up to two moves more than the minimum in each category but marks are deducted if they go over this. The ISU also states that points are to be deducted from both the technical merit and artistic impression marks if there is a lack of connecting steps.

This decision has had an immediate beneficial impact on choreography. Elena Valova and Oleg Vasiliev, USSR, presented some unusual positions and delightful footwork to win the 1983 title on their first World Championship appearance. It was a debut unmatched since Rodnina and Ulanov exploded into international skating in 1969. Significantly perhaps, Valova and Vasiliev are from Leningrad where the importance of choreography has never been completely forgotten and where traces of the Protopopovs' philosophy of pair skating still remain. They made the judges and spectators alike sit up with amazement when, at the beginning of their routine in 1983, they whipped off perfectly matched triple toe loops. No woman had tried a triple toe loop in a World Championship before 1974 when Christine Errath of East Germany won the singles title after falling on that move. Pairs usually confine themselves to far easier solo jumps. Irina Rodnina was the first woman to do a double axel in a pairs programme and many pairs still do not include this jump, which is less difficult than the triple.

Underhill and Martini execute their upside-down lift

One of the balletic poses presented by Oleg Vasiliev and Elena Valova

Not surprisingly, since pair skaters are required to perform so many spins and jumps independently from but in unison with their partners, most are good solo skaters and some have done well in singles competition. More would enter were it not for the school figures requirement. Both Randy Gardner and Tai Babilonia, while they were pair champions, reached sixth place in the US singles championships. Ken Shelley won both the US pairs and men's title in 1972 and finished third and seventh in those categories in the World Championships that year. Tina Reigel of West Germany won a place in both the women's and pair teams for the 1980 European Championships, but had to withdraw from the first event because of illness. She and her partner, Andreas Nischwitz, were third in the 1981 World Championship before their partnership ended through injury when she was only sixteen.

In Britain the promising brother and sister team, Lisa and Neil Cushley, have won five national titles between them, and expect to win more. They have been the British primary and junior pairs champions, Neil has been the British primary and junior boys' champion, and Lisa has been the British primary girls' champion. In December 1982, at the tender age of thirteen and fifteen respectively, they were second in the British senior pair championship and Neil was third in the British senior men's championship, a slot which Robin Cousins held when he was also fifteen.

Lifts are one area in which pair skaters can show their ingenuity, although the ISU has imposed some restrictions on them. The man cannot hold the woman's legs in a lift. She must always be turning while in the air, and when she is fully airborne, with her arms in the locked position, the man cannot turn more than three revolutions.

Adagio spins, a highly popular feature of professional ice shows in which the man spins the woman around him at great speed so that no part of her body touches the ice, are illegal in amateur skating. The US champions, Kitty and Peter Carruthers, aroused a lot of criticism at the 1983 World Championship by including in their practice periods an illegal flip-over death spiral in which Peter yanked Kitty off the ice, turning her over. They left this manoeuvre out of their competition routine, but all the same it looked as if some judges had marked them as if the move had remained in, and they dropped to fourth in world standings, a place lower than the previous year.

The Carruthers have invented two lifts – the lateral twist, similar to the normal twist lift, except that the woman is completely horizontal above her partner's head instead of vertical; and the hydrant lift in which the woman soars over her partner like the whoosh of water from a fire hydrant. The Canadian champions, Barbara Underhill and Paul Martini, have adopted the lateral twist and have developed their own lift in which the woman is held completely upside down in the air.

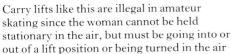

Carry lifts like this are illegal in amateur skating since the woman cannot be held stationary in the air, but must be going into or out of a lift position or being turned in the air

The Toddys do a spectacular adagio spin – a move that is illegal in amateur skating – to win the World Professional Championship, a yearly event which takes place in Jaca, Spain

A backward inside death spiral is always well received by the audience since it allows the woman to get her head even further down on to the ice than in the backward outside variety and as she comes out of the move her hair is generally prettily adorned with a crown of ice flakes. The Protopopovs invented their famous variation of this move, the forward inside death spiral in which the woman circles the man on a forward inside edge, for the 1968–9 season.

The death spiral takes up a large amount of room on the ice in practice and at the 1970 World Championship an incident occurred which led to the reduction of the number of pairs allowed on the ice in each warm-up session. The US champions, Mark and Melissa Militano, were executing a death spiral at the same time as an East German couple were practising flying camels. The East German girl jumped into Melissa's path and had an artery in her leg slashed. Melissa said later she could find no blood on her skates, although it covered the ice, and she felt the injury might have been inflicted by the German boy's blade colliding with his partner as he lost unison in the jump. In any case, the German girl never skated again.

That event, which was held in Ljubljana, Yugoslavia, was particularly bad for Melissa Militano. The day after the accident, in the morning's practice period, on ice that had become very churned up, Mark caught his skate in a rut while holding his sister aloft in an overhead lift. With her hands locked in the hold she was unable to get them into a position to protect her face as she plummeted down, and suffered serious ice burns on her cheek and forehead as a result. She skated that evening looking rather like a reject from a Frankenstein film.

The referee of that championship received a great deal of criticism for another incident which occurred during the free skating event. The Canadian number two team fell during an overhead lift and the woman lay unconscious on the ice for a full minute before recovering and continuing the routine. Many observers felt the referee should have stopped the couple from carrying on, or despatched a doctor on to the ice to check the woman's condition.

Pair skating *can* be dangerous. The accident which kept the British pair champions, Susie Garland and Ian Jenkins, from competing in the World Championship occurred in a collision with another skater during a public session, and that is something which happens all too often. In the USSR, top skaters have the rink to themselves for practice; public skating takes place outdoors and the indoor facilities are reserved for training. There is no National Training Centre in Britain, as there is in East and West Germany, and skaters in this country are obliged, for financial reasons, to practise on crowded rinks. The risks are considerable, and because of this many rink managers will not let pairs skate at all during public sessions.

Kerry Leitch, a top Canadian instructor, insists that all his pupils learn lifts off the ice using pulleys, and that they wear crash helmets when practising new moves to reduce the risk of accident or permanent injury. Leitch tests the young girls who come to him wanting to become pair skaters for fearlessness. He thinks that injury often comes about because the girl tenses up in the wrong place, holding back because she is afraid. If he feels she is too cautious he redirects her into ice dancing or singles so that she, or her potential partner, or Leitch, won't be wasting their time.

Even Irina Rodnina has had her share of accidents. Things were already going badly between her and Alexei Ulanov after he had done a single salchow instead of a double in the short programme section of the 1972 Olympic Games in Sapporo. (All eyes were on Rodnina and, fortunately for them, most of the judges and spectators failed to spot the error.) Ulanov's mind was on Ludmila Smirnova, of the Russian number two pair. Smirnova and her partner Andrei Suraikin took the silver medals, but were immediately sent back to Leningrad, despite the IOC's request that all the medal-winning figure skaters should give exhibitions in the closing ceremonies. In the short time between the Games and the World Championships at Calgary, Ulanov travelled from his home in Moscow to Leningrad to marry Smirnova. Competing with their same partners at Calgary, and assigned the same practice periods, Ulanov – perhaps distracted by his blonde wife – dropped Rodnina from an overhead lift onto her head. She suffered concussion and was kept overnight in a Canadian hospital, but refused to withdraw from the event.

In her autobiography, *Uneven Ice*, written many years later, Rodnina has said the whole competition seemed to pass by in a haze. It was Rodnina and Ulanov's last appearance together. He moved to Leningrad and competed with Smirnova, winning silver medals in the international championships in 1973 and 1974 before joining a Russian ice show. Rodnina thought her career was over, and despaired because she did not have the education to become a coach. Her coach, Stanislav Zhuk, refused to admit defeat, however. He arranged for the use of a Moscow rink for a week while auditions for a new partner took place. Men were brought in from every part of the USSR. Alexander Zaitsev, from Leningrad, three years Rodnina's junior, won the competition. He had competed in pairs before but only in a minor way, and was so in awe of his new partner, he would stutter when she spoke to him. However, the partnership gelled well and in their first international appearance, the 1973 European Championship, they scored a record number of sixes – a record that stood until Torvill and Dean's success in the 1982 European Championships.

Their first World Championship a few weeks later was even more remarkable. Halfway through their performance their music stopped. Zhuk signalled them to continue, defying the referee's obvious gestures.

Rodnina and Zaitsev take a break in practice. Irina watches her former partner, Alexei Ulanov, skate with his new partner and wife, Ludmila Smirnova

Amazingly they ended at exactly the moment the electronic timing device indicated they would have done had the music been playing. The judges marked them as if the music had played, which created much controversy. The second mark in free skating is for artistic impression. Part of it should reflect the way the skaters move to their music. Since there was no music for half the performance, Rodnina and Zaitsev should not have received the high marks they did. They won that event and were never beaten in competition. However, the referee disappeared from the ISU for a decade before reappearing as an international judge at the 1983 World Junior Championships. Other skaters who competed during that period said they had seen slashes on Zaitsev's chest in the dressing room. The marks were from Rodnina's skates cutting him while they were learning the split triple twist lift.

When a partnership breaks up in the West it is not possible to go to the lengths the Russians do to form a new pair. Susie Garland and Robert Daw, who had represented Britain in the 1980 Winter Olympic Games, where they were the youngest competitors, dissolved their partnership partly because Garland had broken a bone in her wrist after falling from a throw move, partly because she was outgrowing Daw, and partly because of personality clashes. She teamed up with the man from the British number two pair, Ian Jenkins, leaving his partner out in the cold. The powerful but stocky Daw remained in the United States in Wilmington where they had been training with his stepmother. He did not find a suitable partner for almost fifteen months. When he did team up with Gillian Wachsman, they did extremely well, gaining fourth place in the 1983 US championship and being picked as first reserves for the US team for that year's World Championship. Because Daw had represented Britain in Lake Placid, however, they were not eligible for the American team at Sarajevo.

Another British skater, Colin Taylforth, found a new partner in a very unusual way. After Linda Connolly, with whom he had competed in the 1972 Olympic Games, had retired and another brief partnership had broken up, Taylforth, desperate for a top-level partner, advertised for one in a skating magazine. Erika Susman, an extremely pretty Californian, replied at once. She had been fourth in the US championships but her partner had turned professional. John Nicks, Susman's coach, arranged for Colin to go to Los Angeles for a try out. It worked, and the only problem in their way now was nationality: if they were to compete in the British championships, Erika needed to acquire British citizenship. This she did by marrying Taylforth, her family raising no objection to their teenaged daughter marrying someone she had only known for a matter of weeks. They won the British title easily. However, while representing Britain in the 1976 Olympic Games, Erika dislocated her shoulder. Their partnership dissolved, and eventually the marriage was annulled.

6

Ice Dance

For many years ice dance was the poor relation of the other skating categories, but on its acceptance into the Olympic programme in 1976 the sport was changed. Before that, ice dancers in countries other than Britain were often failed pairs or singles skaters, and ice dancing had the image of a leisure-time activity pursued by middle-aged ladies with time on their hands and dance instructors who catered to their whims. Certainly the performances of Torvill and Dean, requiring enormous amounts of athletic prowess, have altered that image for all time.

In many countries, ice dancing is now the most popular of the four World Championship events. In Scandinavia, where singles and pair skating are poorly attended, arenas are sold out for the ice dance contest. Betty Callaway, who has taught many champions including Jayne Torvill and Christopher Dean, feels this is possibly because ice dancing is more 'accessible' than pairs and singles, in which the competitors are very young. The audience can identify with the dancers. They can imagine themselves waltzing around this frozen ballroom. The singles and pairs are obviously executing such difficult moves that no such identification can occur.

The ice dance contest is in three sections: three compulsory dances, each worth 10 per cent, the original set pattern dance (OSP), worth 20 per cent, and the free dance, worth 50 per cent. When two couples finish with the same penalty points, then the standings in the free dance are used to break the tie (see chapter 8).

Initially the compulsory dances were worth 60 per cent and no restrictions were placed on the free dance. Competitors could do any move shown by the pairs. However, the ISU soon decided the two events should be more sharply differentiated, and imposed many limitations. For example, in their $3\frac{1}{2}$-minute free dance, competitors were allowed only five small lifts in which the man's hands could not go above his waist, and were not permitted to spin more than one-and-a-half revolutions. As Lawrence Demmy who, with Jean Westwood, won the first four World titles, has said, the event became very dull.

In the late 1960s an OSP dance was included. Contestants had to make up their own 'compulsory' which fitted all the limitations of that category. At first no rhythm was set, but judges found it extremely difficult to compare, say, a slow waltz and a quick polka. Now rhythms are selected for all events for the entire season.

An extra thirty seconds was added to the free dance section a few years ago and, for the 1983 season, the confining technical restrictions were eased a little. The most important change was that the man could now bring his hands up to his shoulders in lifts. Many of the movements Torvill and Dean introduced in their 'Barnum on Ice' routine would not have been possible the year before. Not changed were the regulations stating that toe work should be kept to a minimum. Skates have teeth at the front of the blade. It is possible for even a novice skater to stand on these teeth and do almost anything that can be done on a stage – it requires no skating skill, merely strong ankles.

Professional skaters use the teeth of their skates a great deal when performing on tanks where space is extremely limited and if they used the full edge power and speed of their blades, they might rocket into the audience. This has happened. On an ice rink there is no such excuse. Judges' interpretations of what constitutes a minimum of toe work varies, and officials have hesitated to penalise the skaters who are the worst offenders, the Russians, because in other areas they have contributed so much to the development of the sport.

In the 1970s they brought a freshness to ice dancing by making use of ballet and other dance company choreographers to work on a total presentation. Before the Russians won their first World ice dance championship in 1970, a title they were to keep in the USSR for a decade, skaters concentrated on their footwork and ignored facial expressions and upper body moves. However, these choreographers were not skaters and the variations they thought up, though extremely enjoyable to watch, were

The 1976 Olympic champions, Ludmila Pakhomova and Alexander Gorshkov

Andrei Bukin tosses Natalia Bestemianova around in this exciting move

transposed stage movements, which were sometimes so difficult as to be impossible to do on the blade. Torvill and Dean, by contrast, do all their own choreography which means they can adopt their skating expertise to create novel moves. Outside the USSR most skaters make up their own routines but rely on stylists to give advice on arm placement.

Ludmila Pakhomova, who with her husband, Alexander Gorshkov, was the first Russian to win a World ice dance title and, in 1976, won the first Olympic gold medal ever given for ice dancing, has paid Torvill and Dean the compliment of saying that they could never be beaten. She indicated that the Russians had won for so long because their presentation was vastly superior to that of other couples, who had better technique. Once Torvill and Dean combined their faultless technique with a level of presentation to match the Russians, they had ascended to an unbeatable peak. Unable to skate in the 1983 European Championship because of Torvill's injured shoulder, their title was claimed by Natalia Bestemianova and Andrei Bukin, of the USSR. That victory received a great deal of criticism from, among others, Angelika and Erich Buck – European champions in 1972 – who said that 80 per cent of what the Russians did in their free dance section could have been accomplished in a theatre, and therefore could not be called ice dancing.

Watching the free dance

Ice dance is not a speed contest, but the better skaters are readily apparent by their superior speed and their obvious greater projection of security. There is no place for falls in ice dancing. While singles and pair skaters often sweep the ice with various parts of their anatomy, ice dancers rarely fall.

Torvill and Dean have never fallen in competition, though Dean did sit down unexpectedly in the warm-up for the second compulsory dance in the 1982 World Championship. He later joked that there had been a long time between the two dances, and the fall certainly jerked him out of the stupor into which he had slipped. Karen Barber and Nicky Slater, the second-ranked British ice dance couple, fell for the first time in their competitive career during the OSP division of the 1983 World Championship. Slater was so mortified by this error he went into a state of shock. Barber said it took her much longer than it should have to get him back into the routine.

The US champions, Judy Blumberg and Michael Seibert, however, are very prone to falls, possibly because they do everything at breakneck speed. They lost the bronze medals in the 1981 World Championship because of a bad fall in their free dance, and Blumberg tripped on her final steps in the 1983 US championship – which did not prevent a rather partisan judging panel from awarding the couple five sixes, making a mockery of the perfection that a six is supposed to represent. It should be

Karen Barber and Nicky Slater show excellent form in the Kilian compulsory

Karen Barber and Nicky Slater perform a well-received exhibition move.

readily apparent that the best ice dancers certainly interact with each other, keeping in touch with and looking at their partners. However, they should also look at the audience, bringing them into the performance. Because Barber and Slater train at Richmond, a rink with a small seating capacity, their coach, Jimmy Young, arranged for them to spend some time before the 1983 European Championship, and again before the World Championship, at the arena in Garmisch in West Germany specifically because he felt it would help them to project their performance. He wanted them to make even the people sitting in the last row of the audience feel they were skating for them.

Unison is, of course, another yardstick by which ice dance couples are judged, just as it is in pair skating. It has been said that Torvill and Dean move as if they are four legs attached to one body. They skate very close to each other, something which makes all the moves more difficult. If skaters want to criticise other ice dancers they say there was room to fit another person between them. Poor ice dancers have both legs on the ice a great deal of the time, and tend to progress in straight lines instead of curves.

Ice dancers must interpret their music. Occasionally you will notice a couple, generally newcomers, who have devised a clever move and present it even though it does not fit the music. They are required to

The Canadian champion, Brian Orser, performs his Pink Panther routine (page 67)
Rosalynn Sumners, the 1983 World champion, demonstrates a sit spin (page 69)

Audiences everywhere loved Judy Blumberg and Michael Seibert's Fred Astaire and Ginger Rogers' routine in 1983, but the judges gave the thumbs down

Irina Moiseeva and Andrei Minenkov in one of their extremely expressive performances

demonstrate various moods and are allowed three cuts in their music – that is, four different pieces. The time-honoured method was to pick four tunes that were as varied as possible to show off the skaters' versatility. Naturally that could, and does, cause some very grating changes. In the 1969 season, when Diane Towler and Bernard Ford won the last of their four World championships, they broke new ground by using music from only one source, the film, *Zorba the Greek*. They created a marvellous routine, the highlight of which was an extremely quick portion in which they traversed the length of the rink continuously turning away from each other and briefly touching each other's hands between turns.

Irina Moiseeva and Andrei Minenkov, USSR, almost a decade later, in the 1978 season, skated to a single piece of music, taken from *West Side Story*. Ignoring the film's plot, they finished their four minutes with Moiseeva dying artistically draped on Minenkov's knee as he moved slowly and dramatically around the rink. Unfortunately, they held the pose a little too long at the World Championship and collapsed in an untidy heap with their expressions of great tragedy marred by surprise.

That cost them their title, and although they continued to compete until 1982 they could not recapture their former glory.

Torvill and Dean's use of the uncut overture to *Mack and Mabel* in 1982 took the choice of music to a new height. However, the chances of finding another piece of music which doesn't need cutting, yet contains the necessary changes of mood, are slim. Their use of music that had been specially recorded for them in their 'Barnum' routine was not without precedent. As early as 1936, Herber and Baier of Germany skated to specially composed music to win the pairs' Olympic gold medal; and so did Irina Rodnina and Alexander Zaitsev for their short programme routine in 1975. Not many skaters have such opportunities. However, Linda Fratianne, USA, the 1977 and 1979 women's world champion, turned down an offer by her uncle, Henry Mancini, to compose a special piece for Olympic season in 1980, on the grounds that if the music became very popular her amateur status might be compromised.

Some couples struggle for a spot in the limelight by trying the unusual. The 1983 Canadian champions, Tracy Wilson and Bob McCall, interpreted *War and Peace* for their free dance, which, unsurprisingly, was not as successful as their highly applauded Cool Cat Rock and Roll number had been. Another rising couple, Lisa Spitz and Scott Gregory, USA, have made a name for themselves by spoofing a tango. Judy Blumberg and Michael Seibert presented routines in both the 1982 and 1983 seasons which evoked the Ginger Rogers and Fred Astaire period, even including a section in which they appeared to tap dance. The judges turned their thumbs down because, though they conjured up the image of the big musical film brilliantly, the routines weren't difficult enough.

What this boils down to is that ice dancing, in which the free dance routine is marked in two categories, the first for technical merit and the second for artistic impression, is judged even more subjectively than singles or pair skating, and between couples of relatively equal ability your opinion is just as good as that of the judging panel.

When cornered, judges stress that their marks reflect flow over the ice and deep edges – basically the speed and lean the skaters are able to maintain when on one foot. However, in almost every ice dance competition there are judging controversies, such as the famous one at the 1970 World Championship when Mollie Phillips, the British official, sided with the Communist bloc judges to give the decision to Ludmila Pakhomova and Alexander Gorshkov over the US champions, Judy Schwomeyer and James Sladky. Sladky's bottom stuck out, she said when pressed for an explanation.

Original Set Pattern Dance

For the OSP dance, couples devise a set of steps to fit the rhythm specified by the ISU for that season. These should be designed to take

Brian Boitano, winner of the 1983 Skate America contest, is expected to succeed Scott Hamilton as US champion in January 1985 (page 68)

There is no doubt Toller Cranston would have done better as an amateur if his school figures had been stronger (page 80)

Scott Hamilton's charisma is such that he can carry off an outfit like this! (page 71)

Muscle tension and power are clearly seen as Elaine Zayak performs a spin (page 73)

them completely around the rink. Once they have returned to their skating point, they repeat the steps exactly in the same places on the ice twice, so that when they have finished they have progressed around the rink three times. No lifts are allowed and skaters cannot cross the centre line of the rink, except at the ends, nor circle around on themselves.

The OSP is marked in two categories. The first mark, for composition, takes in the novelty and the difficulty of the steps; the second, for presentation, how well they did them. Three new dances later adopted by the ISU into the compulsory schedule have emerged from this section: the Yankee Polka, created by Schwomeyer and Sladky; the Tango Romantica, created by Pakhomova and Gorshkov; and the Ravensburger Waltz, created by Angelika and Erich Buck. All three had to be changed slightly first: the Ravensburger Waltz by being slowed down, and the other two by having certain steps simplified. Pakhomova and Gorshkov also did a Rhumba OSP which was briefly but unsuccessfully considered for the compulsory schedule. There is no way that even a simplified version of Torvill and Dean's Cha Cha, their 1982 Summertime Blues, or the 1983 Rock and Roll, could be made into compulsories. Their OSPs are just too difficult.

For the 1984 Olympic Games, and for all senior and junior competitions that season, the OSP will be a Paso Doble in 2/4 time and from 52 to 60 bars a minute. In 1985 the rhythm will be the Quickstep, in 2/4 time and 56 to 60 bars a minute.

Compulsory Dances

The three former OSP dances incorporated into the compulsory schedule in the mid 1970s caused a lot of consternation, being at first considered much too complicated. However, now they have been blended into the schedule, top-level competitors feel they have brought new life into this section of the event. Before this only one dance had been added since the schedule was set up – the lovely Starlight Waltz devised by Peri Horne, an instructor at the Streatham rink, and Courtney Jones in 1963.

There was an explosion of interest in ice dancing in Britain in the 1930s, arising from the growth in the number of artificial rinks being built. As a result, there was a demand for ice dance competitions, and a need for new dances. Until then, the Waltz and the Kilian, invented at the beginning of the century, were the only dances available. (The Kilian, still on the ISU schedule today, is executed to march music. The man's and the woman's steps are identical and take them halfway around the centre part of the rink at which point they are repeated, to bring the dancers back to their starting place.) The NSA of Great Britain devised several competitions in the 1930s in which contestants were required to make up dances suitable for the general skater to perform. Almost all the dances in the ISU schedule date from that era.

Above: Janet Thompson and Warren Maxwell of Great Britain who were second in the 1977 World Championship

Right: Judy Blumberg and Michael Seibert, the US champions, high kick in their 1983 Rock and Roll number

For many years the ISU had three groups of its nine most difficult dances on the World championship programme. A draw would be made on the eve of the competition to see which group would be skated, which meant that competitors had to be prepared to demonstrate any of the nine dances. However, after complaining that the same group kept being picked out of the hat, the group skated in the previous year's competition was dropped from the draw every time. When the three new compulsories were incorporated in the mid 1970s the dances were divided into four groups, and the group to be used specified in advance – this was to ensure that competitors did not have to learn the complicated steps of all three dances at once, but could introduce themselves gradually to them. However, for the 1984 season the ISU has reinstated the draw on the eve of the contest, to be made from two of the groups, with the other two groups being used the next season.

This means that the top skaters must now practise six compulsories in any one season instead of three. Torvill and Dean say this has added another one-and-a-half hours to their daily practice which, in summer, climbs to seven hours a day. However, by and large, the change is thought to be beneficial to the British who traditionally do well in the compulsories, since they receive a thorough initial training in technique.

In 1984 Group 2, consisting of the Westminster Waltz, the Paso Doble, and the Rhumba, and Group 3, the Starlight Waltz, the Kilian,

Marina Cherkasova and Sergei Shakhrai execute a pair camel in the 1977 European Championship where they won bronze medals. The disparity in their sizes is obvious! (page 82)

Emi Watanabe, the first Japanese woman to win a medal in a World championship (in 1979), seen here giving an unusual and extremely pleasing exhibition

Claudia Kristofics-Binder of Austria, the 1982 European champion, achieves a pretty effect in this catch-foot, pull-up camel spin (page 73)

and the Tango Romantica, are in the draw. In 1985 it will be Group 1, the Viennese Waltz, the Yankee Polka, and the Blues, and Group 4, the Ravensburger Waltz, the Quickstep, and the Argentine Tango.

Once the group has been picked, the order in which the three dances are to be skated is chosen, as well as the order in which the three set pieces of music for each dance will be played. The ISU provides three different tunes played in strict tempo for each dance, and these are used in succession. These same pieces become very monotonous. New music was chosen by the ISU for the 1983 season and the old tapes, which had served their purpose for eight years, were retired. Even so, some competitors preferred the music with which they had become so familiar.

One mark is given for each dance. Great importance is placed on the correct steps and on posture. It is also extremely important to place the steps on the precise spot of the ice detailed by the rule-books and to repeat them exactly over the first pattern. Some of the dances, for instance the Blues, are half-sequence dances in which the steps take the skaters only halfway around the rink, and they must be repeated three times so that two complete circuits of the rink are made. Most of the dances take the skaters completely around the rink, and they must repeat the steps twice more so that they progress completely around the rink three times.

Ruts inevitably develop in the ice since all the competitors are skating over the same area and, because ice dance skates are thinner than those used for the singles event, they can easily get caught in one of them. Kristina Regoeczy of Hungary, dancing with Andras Sallay with whom she later won the 1980 World title, took a bad fall after her blade got caught in a rut during the Kilian in the 1978 European Championship and, as a result, the ice is now resurfaced more frequently. Even so, championship skaters must know when to move the pattern of their dance slightly to one side to minimise this possibility. This competitive knowledge is one of the areas where Betty Callaway has helped Torvill and Dean so much. When they first came under her tutelage, just after they had competed in their first World Championship in 1978, they were unaware of such subtleties. That attention to minor detail has helped them become the champions they are.

7

The Ins and Outs of Competition

Until recently, the World Championships, held early in March, the European Championships, generally at the end of January (a little earlier in Olympic years) and the Olympic Games were the only international championships sanctioned by the ISU. The World Junior Championships, which take place in December (although they are attributed to the following year) were started in 1978; the others have been held since the last century.

All members of the ISU (except South Africa) may enter at least one competitor in each of the championships (the European Championships are restricted to European members only, including the USSR). Two entries per category are allowed from any country that had a skater or couple placed in the top ten in that category at the previous year's championship, and a maximum of three entries if a country had a skater or an ice dance couple placed in the top three, or a pair in the top five, provided one of them is the skater or couple who did so well before.

The quota for Olympic entry is determined by the placings in the previous year's World Championships. So, for the 1984 Olympic Games, Britain is permitted only one entry for the men's and women's singles and the pairs contests because no British skaters finished in the top ten in these categories in the 1983 World Championships, but is allowed three ice dance couples provided the 1983 World champions are part of the team. If Jayne Torvill and Christopher Dean are not entered, then only two British ice dance couples will be allowed.

However, partly because of the loosening of the regulations regarding the sponsorship of events involving amateurs, international events have proliferated in recent years. The season now begins in August with the St Gervais Grand Prix in France and the Nebelhorn Trophy in West Germany, held in consecutive weeks. Although entry to both is not compulsory, a cup is given to the country whose team has acquired the greatest number of points in the two contests. It is most often claimed by Americans whose national association makes a practice of entering youngsters, most of whom have not travelled outside the United States before. The highlight of the trip is generally the six-hour bus trip through the spectacular Alpine scenery between the two towns.

World champions Charlie Tickner (1978), Linda Fratianne (1977 and

Tai Babilonia and Randy Gardner are well known for this spectacular throw move (page 82)

Babilonia and Gardner execute a perfect backward outside death spiral (page 89)

In Lea Ann Miller and Bill Fauver's variation of a pair sit spin she reaches back to grasp her skate with her hand (page 86)

Kitty and Peter Carruthers execute the lateral twist – a move they invented (page 88)

A Zamboni machine scrapes off the top layer of ground-up ice and puts down a layer of hot water which freezes smoothly to remake the ice in a matter of minutes. Previously this would have taken an hour, so that competitions were a good deal more drawn out.

1979) and Tai Babilonia and Randy Gardner (1979) gained their first international experience in these events and were amazed by the strange conditions encountered. In those days, the rinks were still partially out of doors. Fratianne, a matchstick midget of twelve, struggled vainly through her exhibition after winning the Grand Prix. The very warm outside air, mixing with the coldness generated by the ice, formed a dense billowing mist which threatened to engulf her completely. The music her coach had chosen could not have been less suitable. It was 'One Fine Day' from the opera, *Madame Butterfly*. The St Gervais Grand Prix also provided Torvill and Dean, as well as Cousins and Curry, with their first taste of international success. For Curry it was his only international victory before his glorious 1976 season.

In September Austria holds a women's competition in Vienna and, at the end of the month, the St Ivel company sponsors a highly regarded event at the Richmond rink in which several World champions have taken part. The Skate America and Skate Canada contests are scheduled for October at varying sites, while the Ennia Cup, held at the Hague in Holland and consisting only of the free skating sections of the four disciplines, as well as the Prague and Zagreb Internationals, and the Japanese NHK contest, take place in November. A Russian newspaper sponsors an event in Moscow and there is a Blue Swords competition in East Germany, but although these contests are interesting, because they demonstrate the relative merits of the top skaters of those countries, very few Western skaters take part in them. Junior competitions are springing up in most countries and the competition for the best dates is fierce.

With so many contests, organisers fight for the cream of the skaters. Those at the top are constantly inundated with invitations to compete, and if that isn't possible, at least to support the event by giving an exhibition. The ISU controls the amount of money an amateur skater may receive for an exhibition. In 1982 the amount was doubled from the previous sum of 200 Swiss francs. This present is sometimes demanded in advance. Organisers of one of the Skate Canada contests were horrified to discover that the Russian team, which included Irina Rodnina and Alexander Zaitsev, who were there to give exhibitions, would not leave the airport arrival area until they had had their expenses and stipends in cash right there and then.

Like all amateur sports, there are suggestions of under-the-counter payments which should ease up after the trust fund arrangements, already allowed in other sports by the IOC, are brought belatedly into skating. Competitors do acquire some money from the ISU tour of champions which follows the World Championships. The top skaters are required to give twenty or so exhibitions in four weeks, earning an exhibition fee for each, and having their expenses fully paid. However, some skaters, exhausted after a long competitive season, would rather return home immediately after the event. Curry has said that, in the days when the financial rewards for exhibitions were much less, the ISU exploited the skaters. They did not dare to turn down the tour invitation for fear of antagonising officials who might be judging them in the future. In 1976, at the end of his competitive career, both he and Dorothy Hamill walked out halfway through the tour. The ISU now requires all competitors in the World Championships to sign a paper stating that if they win a medal they will agree to go on the tour. Torvill and Dean caused great disappointment to many of their fans when they secretly left the 1983 tour early – the strain, Betty Callaway said, was just too much as Jayne's injured shoulder still needed taping before each performance.

Britain has not held an international championship since 1952. The NSA made an unsuccessful application for the 1986 event and is expected to try again for 1988. The plan calls for two ice surfaces to be laid down in the National Exhibition Centre in Birmingham, with the nearby Solihull rink also used for practice. Entry for the world championships is so large that three rinks are needed to accommodate the necessary practice schedules. All competitions are subject to a host of ISU regulations developed over the years and covering everything from the starting and finishing

Kitty and Peter Carruthers in their famous 'hydrant' lift (page 88)

Barbara Underhill and Paul Martini's magnificent forward inside death spiral (page 89)

This balletic pose shows the good use Elena Valova and Oleg Vasiliev have made of choreography (page 87)

times to the provisioning of pencils for the referee. At the draw for the skating order for the initial sections there is even a draw to see which country shall draw first.

In 1982 the huge entry required that the school figures contests for men and women start at 6 am. The reigning champion, Scott Hamilton, had to be up well before then since he had drawn to skate in the first group, and the bus ride to the suburban Copenhagen rink took half an hour. To prevent this happening again the international championship schedule was expanded by a day in 1983. Now all international championships except for the Olympics start with the draws on a Sunday and finish the following Sunday afternoon with an exhibition programme given by the skaters who did best in the event.

The actual competition begins on Monday morning at 8 am with either the men's or the women's school figures, a slow-moving musicless section which takes many hours to complete. Before the event's first official practice one of the two figure groups set by the ISU for all senior contests for the whole season was drawn, and now the draw to decide the starting foot is made. Although skaters are expected to be equally agile on either foot in school figures, a sigh of relief generally goes up when the right foot is drawn, meaning that two of the three figures, the first and the third, will have a right-foot start.

In recent years, for economic reasons, the school figure sections at international championships have been held in a smaller arena than the one for the free skating, since there are very few spectators. When the free skating is televised, the film technicians like the ice to be a brilliant white. However, since television is not interested in figures, the ice surface can be much duller, thus enabling the skater to see his or her tracings more easily and making errors more visible for the judges.

To this end the figure rink for the 1976 Olympic Games consisted of Wedgwood blue ice. However, in Tokyo at the 1977 World Championships, a near disaster occurred when the officials tried to produce similarly coloured ice. The paint had not dried sufficiently before an attempt was made to build up the surface, and it ran. When the ISU officials first went into the arena they were confronted with an ice surface which looked like an ocean. The blue paint had separated, to give the illusion of waves. One judge said she would definitely get seasick if made to stand on this surface. The ice had to be taken up and new paint, this time black, laid down, and the ice again built up. The skaters performed on a dark grey surface that proved satisfactory for the figures. There were other problems with this arena which BBC commentator Alan Weeks found to his cost. He tripped over a hole and broke an ankle.

Skaters are not allowed to use markings on the ice, such as ice hockey lines, to line up the figures they draw on the virgin ice, but the experienced skater knows how to use points of reference without making them too obvious. If a competitor tries to make too blatant use of some marking the referee stops the skater before he gets started and asks him to choose another piece of the ice.

Choosing the best portion of ice can be critical. All ice surfaces have some imperfections, slight hills and dales which can affect the speed of travel as the skater proceeds at snail's pace around his circles. A down slope can be utilised to help return a skater to his start. A small hill in the wrong place can prove disastrous. An up-and-coming skater will often choose to do his figure right next to that of the champion to emphasise the fact that, although he may not be well known, his figures are comparable to those of the established star.

In all but the paragraph figures, the skater does three tracings on each foot placed as precisely as possible one on top of the other. (In the paragraph figures the ISU recently deemed that two tracings were enough and this has helped speed up contests.) In Sonja Henie's day the judges held up their marks immediately after the skater had finished the figure. Nowadays they spend up to several minutes walking around the figure, pacing across the circles to check that they are equally sized and then examining the turns for the tell-tale second line that indicates a dreaded 'flat' (when both edges of the blade touched the ice at the same time).

Robin Cousins performs a school figure in front of the judges. The referee carries a brush to sweep away snow thrown up by the skating blade during a turn so that the judges can see the tracing more clearly

After the skater completes a school figure the referee places marker poles at each turn. Here the judges, including the Russian official Igor Kabanov (number 3), examine a turn. The boxes they carry contain the marks they will shortly hold up.

The 'bowl' spin variation of the pair sit spin developed by Lea Ann Miller and Bill Fauver (page 86)

The favourites to win the 1984 World Championship, Barbara Underhill and Paul Martini, in a tabletop lift (page 88)

Lea Ann Miller looks at the ice as she and Bill Fauver demonstrate their variation of the back inside death spiral (page 89)

Andrei Bukin says that his wife and former partner doesn't mind him skating with the fiery, expressive Natalia Bestemianova – as long as he brings home the medals (page 95)

Most skaters leave the ice after performing their figure, grimacing and shaking their heads. Peggy Fleming was not a believer in that approach. At the height of her career, after completing a figure before judges, she would take a few seconds to assess her tracings. She would then break into a smile and nod to her coach. Psychologically this must have put the judges in the right frame of mind to award good marks.

Before the first skater's marks are held up, the referee asks the judges privately for their marks. He, or she, then feeds back to the judges the highest, the lowest, and the average mark and, at this point only, they are permitted to change their mark. This is to prevent one judge marking unduly highly, or lowly, throughout the event and being continually applauded or booed. Changing marks is not permitted at any point after this. This procedure is enforced in all competition categories.

Spectators at figure events walk around carefully so as not to make any sudden noise which might disturb the skater. The cold silence is similar to a cathedral hush. At the Olympic Games, however, an unfamiliar sound breaks the calm – the noise of camera shutters. Since this section is usually so quiet – newspaper photographers generally confine themselves to the free skating – this re-echoing intrusion can be extremely off-putting and it is a wise coach who prepares his charge so that he or she is not unsettled by this unexpected media interest.

So that the same skaters do not have to perform first in all three figures, the competitors are divided into three groups. The group that executed the first figure first is placed at the end for the second figure. The original middle group of skaters now executes the second figure first and is placed last for the third figure. This also applies to the compulsory dance draw. It means that the skaters who did the first figure in the first group have a long wait until their turn comes for the second figure.

Cynthia Coull and Mark Rowsom of Canada have worked with a sports psychologist who has taught them to seek out faces in the crowd as they take the ice. This helps them not only to relate to the audience but to shut out the marks of the previous pair, so preventing them from becoming more nervous.

The draw for the next section – the short programme, or the OSP division in the ice dance competition – is made immediately after the results of the school figures, or the compulsory dance section, have been announced. Although working out the results is complicated, the widespread use of computers now means that they are available almost immediately. The draw is open to the public to ensure no hanky panky goes on, and at least one official and one competitor must be present. Most skaters attend the draw because it is the fastest way of finding out the results of the just completed section.

No more than eight skaters are allowed in the warm-up for the short programme and so the skaters are divided into groups of eight or less. The draw is made within these groups and is done so that the lower-placed skaters compete first. If there are thirty competitors, for instance, the short programme section begins with the seven skaters who were placed last in the figures, performing in the order which they have drawn amongst themselves. Then the next lowest group of seven skaters perform, then the next eight, and finally the eight who have done best.

For the free skating the maximum number of skaters in a warm-up is six and so the number of skaters is divided into groups of six or less. When it is necessary to have some groups with a lesser number of skaters than other groups, the bigger groups always skate last. For instance, if there were twenty-one skaters for the free skating, the groups would be of five, five, five, and finally six skaters. The draw for the free skating used to be done on the results of the short programme alone. However, for the 1983 season the system was changed so that the draw was done on the combined result of the school figures and the short programme, and if there were more than twenty-four competitors only the top fifteen were allowed to skate in the 'A' final, with the rest of the competitors having a run-off at a different time. This has proved extremely unpopular and Norbert Schramm, the 1982 and 1983 European champion, has become the unofficial spokesman for the skaters in making their feelings felt about this situation.

The ISU has said that no change can be considered before the summer of 1984. Because the schedule was set so far in advance, the Olympic Games will be conducted under the old method. In this a poor school figures exponent, if he does brilliantly in the short programme, can win a position to free skate with the top group. The new system keeps relatively poor free skaters in the top group by virtue of their school figures prowess. Since school figures and free skating demand very different abilities, the new system denies the skater who was lying sixteenth the chance to climb into the top ten, which was quite feasible before.

The same panel of nine judges marks all three sections of an event. If the judges' marks differ by one full point (that is ten-tenths) then the referee has the right to stop the contest and call a huddle in which both

Tracy Wilson and Bob McCall in their 'Cool Cat' Rock and Roll number (page 99)

Ludmila Pakhomova and Alexander Gorshkov won the first Olympic gold medals awarded for dancing in 1976 (page 95)

Kristina Regoeczy and Andras Sallay, the Hungarian champions who trained with Betty Callaway (page 106)

Irina Moiseeva and Andrei Minenkov, World champions in 1975 and 1977. They did not appreciate their nicknames of Min and Mo, given them by Western journalists (page 98)

the judge who gave the highest mark and the judge who gave the lowest mark are asked for an explanation. If the referee deems these are not sufficient the judges are asked to give a written explanation and the referee can advise the ISU to suspend an erring judge for incompetence or national bias. Referees tend to be very lenient, however. In the 1982 World Championship the Hungarian champions pulled out of the ice dance contest just before it started. One judge did not notice this, although all competitors' names are called before they skate and judges are required to watch practice periods and make themselves familiar with the skaters. Instead of the Hungarians the next competitors, the third-ranked Russians, performed the compulsory dance and received high marks from all but the Austrian judge, who presented the low mark which the Hungarians would probably have received. This obvious pre-marking was allowed to pass by uncriticised.

In addition to the medals for overall performances, since 1973 smaller medals are awarded in a private ceremony for the top three skaters in the school figures, and for the top three in the combined short programme section and the free skating.

All the judges must be amateurs. Until recently an international judge needed only to have his national association put forward his name. To help counter incidents of incompetence, the ISU now insists that all judges new to international experience take part in seminars which are usually held in conjunction with the World Championships and make use of skaters who have taken part in that event to demonstrate moves and faults. This has considerably improved the level of judging, but there are still unfortunate incidents. One long-serving West German judge was discovered to be almost blind. The revelation came when he was turned down for a driving licence after failing his eye-test even wearing glasses. For a while the ISU contemplated establishing an upper age limit for judges. However, most judges from the West are only able to devote so much time to the sport because they are retired and can afford the time for the necessary travel.

To reach the position of international judge all officials have for years endured early morning starts and long hours standing in intensely cold rinks encouraging medium and lesser talented children while fending off the barbs of enraged parents and unappreciative coaches. By the time they have reached international status, with its travel privileges and first class accommodation, they can be forgiven for wishing to hold on to their positions of power for as long as possible, sometimes even after they are no longer capable of carrying out their responsibilities fully. However, if the spectators suspected this of a particular judge, it might persuade them to be more hearty with their disapproval, for it is a rare competition in which the audience fails to show its appreciation of the judging in the form of boos.

8

Working out the Results

In July 1980 a new method of calculating final results was adopted by the ISU, to apply to all skating competitions. What happens is that the skater's position in each section of the competition is multiplied by a specific factor and these numbers are added together. The winning skater is the one with the lowest 'penalty points'. In the case of a tie, the skater who has been placed higher in the free skating, or the couple who has been placed higher in the free dance, is given the higher overall standing.

In singles contests the school figures, and in the ice dance competitions the compulsory dances, are worth 30 per cent of the total event, and the multiplication factor for these portions is 0.6. The short programme in the singles contests, and the OSP in the ice dance competitions, are worth 20 per cent, and the multiplication factor is 0.4. The free skating and the dance are worth 50 per cent and the multiplication factor for these is 1.0. Pair competitions comprise only two sections, the short programme and the free skating. The skaters' place in the former is multiplied by 0.4 and added to their position in the free skating.

In the 1983 World Ice Dance Championship Jayne Torvill and Christopher Dean won all three sections, and so they received the minimum possible penalty points, 2.0. That was computed as $(1 \times 0.6) + (1 \times 0.4) + (1 \times 1)$. Natalia Bestemianova and Andrei Bukin, USSR, were third in the compulsory dances and OSP sections but gained second place in the free dancing by the finest of margins. They were second with $(3 \times 0.6) + (3 \times 0.4) + (2 \times 1) = 5.0$ penalty points. Judy Blumberg and Michael Seibert, USA, had been clearly second in the first two portions but were placed marginally below the Russians in the free dance. Their score was computed $(2 \times 0.6) + (2 \times 0.4) + (3 \times 1)$, and although they ended up with 5.0, the same number of penalty points, the tie was broken in favour of the Russians because they were placed higher in the free dance.

Before this system was adopted an extremely complicated method was used. Each judge's marks were kept separately. These marks were multiplied by a specific factor and added to that judge's marks for the next section after those had been multiplied by a different factor. The 'majority' system (still in use for working out the results for each individual section) was then applied to compute the final results. The results took a long time to work out and, because a far greater spread of marks is used in

Judy Blumberg and Michael Seibert in one of their extrovert dance routines (page 95)

Out of the shadow at last – Nicky Slater and Karen Barber in the Charlie Chaplin routine that won them the 1983 St Ivel ice dance championship (page 95)

judging the school figures than the free skating, a 'weighting' in favour of the good figure skaters occurred. Good free skaters were saddled with deficits they could not overcome.

The new system with its reverse 'sudden death' weighting in favour of the free skating and free dance sections puts more pressure on skaters like Torvill and Dean. No matter how superior they are in the compulsory dances and OSP divisions, they cannot establish a cushioning margin of safety. If the couple who were second in both these initial sections beat them in the free dance by as little as a hair's breadth, then Torvill and Dean would be second overall.

This system has been highly criticised by Norbert Schramm, reflecting the thoughts of most competitive skaters. He does not like skaters being placed in the position that, no matter how brilliantly they perform, they

Elaine Zayak, the 1982 World champion, discovered some of the tricks of competition early in her career. When she was eleven, someone asked her why she was in the locker room continually flushing all the toilets. She replied that she was drowning out the sound of the other skaters' marks so that they could not discourage her

Norbert Schramm in typical exuberant posture. Like Cousins, Schramm – a soldier in the West German army – is weak in the school figures. This cost him the 1981 and 1982 German championships, won by Heiko Fischer

cannot win unless the judges put another skater lower than, say, fourth. He is drawing attention to a particular anomaly which exists because the new system does not reflect whether the difference between skaters' positions are large or small. The increment between second and first, and between every other placing, is always the same. The ISU, while recognising the criticisms, has said no change can be considered before their Congress in the summer of 1984.

The new system has caused problems in national events in which the number of entries is low, as is generally the case with the men's singles contests. Poor school figures exponents have been winning titles when their rivals were slotted into a certain order. For instance, if skater A is first in the school figures and short programme sections but third in the free skating, while skater B is second in all three divisions, and skater C was third in the first two sections but wins the free skating, then skater C will win the event. However, if skater C is chosen for the World championship, he is likely to come thirtieth in the school figures and do less well than skater B whose abilities are consistent in all three sections.

Working out results in each section (the 'majority' system)

From time to time a newcomer to the sport, discovering that a skater who has more marks in a section than another has been given second place in that section, cries 'Fix!' Actually, the 'majority' system is far fairer than a system relying on the mere totalling up of marks, when it is possible, if one judge marks particularly high or particularly low, for him or her to have undue influence on the final result. The 'majority' system is even fairer than the one used in international diving, in which the top and the bottom marks given to each diver are thrown out before calculating the result. The subjective element in the judging of skating has long been acknowledged, particularly when national prejudice is involved. To eliminate the effect of this in international championships a panel of nine judges is used. If the majority, that is five out of nine, decide one skater should win, he or she does win, regardless of the opinions of the other judges. In lesser events, seven, five, or even three judges are used. The marks each judge gives are put in order and given an 'ordinal'. The skater to whom the judge has given his or her highest marks receives a '1' ordinal. The one with the next highest mark gets a '2' ordinal, and so on. The accountants search through the lists for the skater who has a 'majority' of '1' ordinals, and he or she is the winner. However, with a panel of nine judges, if four give a skater '1' ordinals and the rest split their '1's between other skaters, the first skater does not necessarily win. If there is no majority for first place, then the accountants search for those skaters who have at least five votes of second or first, and the skater with the most number of these combined votes wins.

Sometimes a judge will award the same marks to more than one skater.

If this occurs in the short programme, OSP, free skating, or free dance sections, where each judge gives two marks, the first mark is used to break the tie. For instance a 5.8 for technical merit and 5.7 for artistic impression in a free skating performance is better than a 5.7 and 5.8. However, two sets of 5.8s would be given the same ordinal. (In every category, 6.0 is the maximum mark a judge can give.)

An interesting situation occurred in the ice dance event of the 1980 Olympic Games. (This happened when the majority system was used to compute overall results and not just the results in each portion of a championship.) This is how the judges placed the top three competitors:

	FRG	USA	URS	CSR	HUN	AUT	CAN	GRB	FRA
Linichuk/Karponosov (URS)	2	2	1	1	2	1	1	1	2
Regoeczy/Sallay (HUN)	1	1	3	2	1	2	2	1	1
Moiseeva/Minenkov (URS)	3	3	2	3	3	3	3	4	3

The British judge, Brenda Long, had given the Russian and Hungarian couples exactly equal marks and so they were both awarded her '1' ordinal. This meant that both couples had five votes for first place. To break this tie, the accountants, or in this case the computer, had to discover who had the majority of '2' ordinals and better. The Russian judge had given his country's second strings (Moiseeva and Minenkov) his second-place vote, with the result that the Hungarians only had eight

Kristina Regoeczy and Andras Sallay of Hungary missed winning the 1980 Olympic gold medals by a fraction in an unpopular decision. A few weeks later they won the World Championship without difficulty

Judy Blumberg and Michael Seibert performing their 1983 Rock and Roll number

votes for second place or better, and Linichuk and Karponosov nine. The Russians therefore won the Olympic gold medals. Some weeks later, in a backlash against this decision, the Hungarians dethroned the Russians at the World Championship.

In the 1983 World Ice Dance Championship the decision in the free dance section was very close between second and third places. If Blumberg and Seibert had received 0.2 of a point more from either the Italian or Austrian judges for their second mark, for artistic impression, or 0.2 more from the Italian judge for technical merit, then they would have gained another second place vote instead of the Russians, giving them five votes of second instead of four. This would have given the Americans second place in this section and second place overall. This is the table of the free dance marks:

	ITA	SWI	JPN	USA	CAN	AUT	URS	HUN	GRB
Bestemianova/	5.8	5.7	5.8	5.7	5.8	5.7	5.9	5.8	5.8
Bukin (URS)	5.7	5.9	5.8	5.8	5.8	5.8	5.9	5.8	5.7
	11.5	11.6	11.6	11.5	11.6	11.5	11.8	11.6	11.5
	2	3	2	3	3	2	2	2	3
Blumberg/	5.7	5.8	5.7	5.8	5.8	5.7	5.8	5.8	5.8
Seibert (USA)	5.7	5.8	5.8	5.9	5.9	5.7	5.7	5.7	5.8
	11.4	11.6	11.5	11.7	11.7	11.4	11.5	11.5	11.6
	3	2	3	2	2	3	3	3	2

If the Americans had received 0.1 more from the Italian judge for artistic impression the Russians still would have received the Italian's second-place vote and the Americans his third-place vote because the first mark is used to break a tie; so that 5.8 for the first mark plus 5.7 for the second mark is worth more than 5.7 for the first mark and 5.8 for the second mark. If the Japanese judge had given the Americans 0.1 of a point more in the technical merit mark, or the Austrian judge given the Americans 0.1 of a point more for the artistic impression mark, then these judges would have tied the two couples and both would have received their second-place votes. If either the Japanese or the Austrian had done this then both couples would have had five votes for second place. The accountants would then consider all the judges' votes, and this too would have produced a tie. In this case the marks of all the judges would be totalled, and the Russians would have got the decision. The Russian judge had given his couple 0.3 of a mark over the Americans and this would have swayed the decision. It can be seen that, although the system tries to eliminate national prejudice, in tight decisions it sometimes can affect the final result.

The results can change unexpectedly. In the 1979 European Championships there was almost a three-way tie for first place between the Russian, Vladimir Kovalev, the East German, Jan Hoffmann, and Robin Cousins. Jean-Christophe Simond of France had drawn to skate last and stood no chance of getting into the top three. Just before the Frenchman skated the placings were:

	URS	GDR	HUN	FRG	AUT	CSR	POL	FRA	GRB
Kovalev (URS)	1	2	2	3	2	1	2	2	3
Hoffmann (GDR)	3	1	3	1	1	2	1	3	2
Cousins (GRB)	2	3	1	2	3	3	3	1	1

No skater had a majority of five or more votes for first place, so the skater with the most second or better places had to be determined. The Russian had seven, the East German six, and Cousins five. This was the way the contest was expected to finish; Kovalev first, Hoffmann second, and Cousins third. Since the event was running late, Dutch television went off the air having assured their viewers that Kovalev was the champion. Every reporter except those from France had started dictating their stories back to their papers over the phone.

However, Simond had a brilliant night. His high marks for the free skating changed the overall positions of the French and British judges. The French official put Simond second overall, which took one of Kovalev's votes of second or better away. This was the key factor. (The English official put Simond third overall which gave Kovalev fourth overall, but this was not to affect the final outcome.) Both the Russian and the East German now had six votes of second or better. To decide

Sabine Baess and Tassilo Thierbach of East Germany demonstrate a double loop lift. Note that Sabine's hands are behind her

Kitty and Peter Carruthers do a variation of a double loop lift in which Kitty's legs are raised

between the two, following the recognised procedure, the sum of these six votes was calculated. Hoffmann's four firsts and two seconds was obviously better than Kovalev's two firsts and four seconds, so the East German was given the title. Pandemonium reigned in the press room when journalists sought to explain this amazing situation briefly. The final table after Simond had skated was like this:

	URS	GDR	HUN	FRG	AUT	CSR	POL	FRA	GRB
Kovalev (URS)	1	2	2	3	2	1	2	3	4
Hoffmann (GDR)	3	1	3	1	1	2	1	4	2
Cousins (GRB)	2	3	1	2	3	3	3	1	1
Simond (FRA)	4	4	4	4	4	4	4	2	3

Though computers are used nowadays, the results are still checked by hand and until the referee has signed the accountant's copy, the results are not official. At one World Championship the referee took the results home with him and they were not declared official until fourteen hours after that event had finished. Fortunately, for the peace of mind of competitors, coaches and parents, that doesn't usually happen. After spending long hours in cold rinks most referees are glad to have the event finalised as soon as possible.

Tracy Wilson and Bob McCall, the 1983 Canadian champions, won world-wide recognition for their 'Cool Cat' Rock and Roll number

Calendar of Events

The European Championships,
Budapest, Hungary, *9–14 January 1984*

The Winter Olympic Games,
Sarajevo, Yugoslavia, *7–19 February 1984*
  Friday 10 February (Zetra Arena)
  Compulsory dances *2–6 pm.*
  Pairs short programme *8–11 pm.*
  Sunday 12 February (Zetra Arena)
  OSP dance *2–6 pm.*
  Pairs free skating (final event) *7.30–11 pm.*
  Monday 13 February (Skenderija Arena)
  Men's school figures *7 am–3 pm.*
  Tuesday 14 February (Zetra Arena)
  Men's short programme *3.30–6.30 pm.*
  Free dance (final event) *7.30 pm–11 pm.*
  Wednesday 15 February (Skenderija Arena)
  Women's school figures *7 am–4 pm.*
  Thursday 16 February (Zetra Arena)
  Women's short programme *2–6.30 pm.*
  Men's free skating (final event) *7.30–11 pm.*
  Saturday 18 February (Zetra Arena)
  Women's free skating (final event) *7–11 pm.*

Sunday 19 February (Zetra Arena) closing
ceremonies which include exhibitions by
all the figure-skating medal winners.

The World Championships,
Ottawa, Canada, *19–24 March 1984*

St Ivel Ice International
London, Great Britain, *24–27 Sep 1984*

The 1985 World Junior Championships,
Colorado Springs, USA, *11–16 Dec 1984*

The 1985 European Championships,
Göteborg, Sweden, *4–9 Feb 1985*

The 1985 World Championships,
Toyko, Japan, *4–9 March 1985*

The 1986 European Championships,
Copenhagen, Denmark, *27 Jan–1 Feb 1986*

The 1986 World Championships,
Geneva, Switzerland, *24 Feb–2 March 1986*

ISU Member Countries

AUS	Australia	ITA	Italy
AUT	Austria	JPN	Japan
BEL	Belgium	LUX	Luxembourg
BUL	Bulgaria	MON	Mongolia
CAN	Canada	NED	Netherlands
CHN	China	NZL	New Zealand
CSR	Czechoslovakia	NOR	Norway
DEN	Denmark	POL	Poland
DPK	North Korea	ROK	South Korea
FRG	Federal Republic of Germany	RUM	Romania
	(West Germany)	SAF	South Africa
FIN	Finland	SPN	Spain
FRA	France	SWE	Sweden
GDR	German Democratic Republic	SWI	Switzerland
	(East Germany)	URS	Union of Soviet Socialist Republics
GRB	Great Britain	USA	United States of America
HUN	Hungary	YUG	Yugoslavia

Two new members were admitted in 1983 – the Chinese Taipei Skating Association *and the* Hong Kong Ice Activities Association

Leading World Skaters

MEN T–Trainer WC–World Championships EC–European Championships OG–Olympic Games WJC–World Junior Championships Ch–Championship ch–champion

Beacom, Gary (CAN)
23.2.60, Toronto.
1983: 13th WC on 1st appearance;
2nd Canadian Ch.
Known for his innovative positions following the direction of Toller Cranston.

Boitano, Brian (USA)
22.10.63, Sunnyvale, Ca.   T. Linda Leaver
1983: 7th WC on 1st appearance; 2nd US Ch.
1982: 4th US Ch; 1st Skate Canada, beating Orser; 1st Ennia Cup, beating Schramm.
1978: 3rd WJC; 1st Vienna Cup.
Started ice skating after wearing out roller skates. Does triple axels with ease, and has done quadruple toe-loop jumps in practice 'with 50% consistency'.

Cerne, Rudi (FRG)
26.9.58, Herne.   T. Gunter Zoeller
1983: 10th WC; 7th EC. *1982:* 15th WC;
4th EC. *1981:* 1st Ennia Cup. *1980:* 11th WC.
1978: 14th WC; 7th EC. West German
ch 1980, 1978.
Has balletic style reminiscent of John Curry, and is extremely pleasing to watch. In Germany

has cult of followers who chant 'Rudi! Rudi! Rudi!' whenever he takes the ice.

Cockerell, Mark (USA)
24.4.62, Burbank, Ca.   T. Betty Berens
1983: 14th WC on 1st appearance;
3rd US Ch.
A flashy free skater and one of the few able to do a triple toe loop to triple toe loop combination of jumps. Weak in school figures and was 19th in this section in 1983 WC.

Fadeev, Alexander (URS)
4.1.64, Tashkent, now Moscow.
1983: 4th WC; 3rd EC. *1982:*
10th WC; 5th EC. *1981:* 9th EC. *1980:*
14th WC; 1st WJC (3rd in 1979). In 1982/3
won Moscow Skates and URS Ch from
Igor Bobrin (1st EC, 3rd WC 1981).
Known for magnificent jumping ability. In both 1983 EC and WC tried quadruple toe loop, which he has landed in practice. In EC executed a triple salchow to triple toe loop combination, and in WC the even more difficult triple lutz to triple toe loop. If he can improve school figures, will undoubtedly be World ch in near future.

Brian Boitano

Mark Cockerell

Alexander Fadeev

Grzegorz Filipowski

Scott Hamilton

Brian Orser

Norbert Schramm

Filipowski, Grzegorz (POL)
28.7.66, Lodz. *T.* Barbara Kossowska
1983: 8th EC, but missed WC because of illness. *1982:* 13th WC; 9th EC. *1981:* 11th WC; 7th EC. *1980:* 15th WC, aged 13, awarded prize for unluckiest skater (German journalists said it must have been for his lack of height and not for his skating ability).
Will undoubtedly be a top competitor after the 1984 OG.

Fischer, Heiko (FRG)
25.2.60, Stuttgart. *T.* Karel Fajfr
1983: 8th WC on 1st appearance; 4th EC; 1st St Ivel. *1982:* 6th EC. West German ch 1983, 1982 and 3rd previously.
Tallest of the men skaters (6' 3''). His rotation in the air has been timed and he is believed to be the fastest of any skater. Strength lies in triple jumps; speciality is triple toe loop to triple toe loop combination.

Hamilton, Scott (USA)
28.8.58, Bowling Green, Ohio, now Denver, Co. *T.* Don Laws
1983, 1982, 1981: 1st WC. *1980:* 5th WC; 5th OG. *1978:* 11th WC. US ch since 1981.
As a child was afflicted with Schwachman's Syndrome, an intestinal paralysis which kept him in hospital for years since he could not absorb nutrients from food. At one point was given nose-drip feedings 6 hours a day and given 6 months to live. The damp atmosphere of ice rinks and his desire for physical activity apparently cured him, though his growth was stunted (he is 5' 3'' and weighs 7 stone 8, 48kg). Noted for his charisma and personality on the ice. In 1983 skated in extremely sombre outfits in attempt to disperse the effeminate, sequinned image of men's figure skating.

Kirsten, Falko (GDR)
3.1.64, Dresden. *T.* Ingrid Lehmann
1983: 12th WC; 12th EC. *1981:* 13th WC; 8th EC. East German ch. Did not compete in 1982.

Kotin, Vladimir (URS)
28.3.62, Moscow. *T.* Elena Tchaikovskaya.
1983: 9th WC; 5th EC. *1982:* 11th WC; 7th EC. *1981:* 9th WC; 6th EC.
A powerful free skater with a mastery of triple jumps.

Orser, Brian (CAN)
18.12.61, Orillia, Ont. *T.* Doug Leigh
1983: 3rd WC. *1982:* 4th WC. *1981:* 6th WC on 1st appearance. Canadian ch since 1981.

Won St Ivel 1982, 1981, both times beating the no. 2 ranked world skater.
Known as Mr Triple Axel from the ease with which he executes this 3½-turn jump. In 1981 was only second skater ever to execute triple axel in WC (after Vern Taylor in 1978). Weak in school figures (8th in 1983 WC, 12th in 1982), and is also criticised that he can only jump and his routines lack artistry. Has done quadruple toe loops in practice and is likely to include them in his routine in the future.

Pepperday, Mark (GRB)
15.3.61, Nottingham. *T.* Wendy Paton
1983: 20th WC; 15th EC. *1982:* 21st WC; 16th EC. *1981:* 14th EC. First won British Ch in Dec. 1981. His sister was British indoor speed ch.

Sabovcik, Josef (CSR)
4.12.63, Bratislava. *T.* Agnesa Burilova
1983: 6th WC; 2nd EC. *1982:* 16th WC; 8th EC. *1981:* 12th WC; 5th EC. *1980:* 16th WC; 9th EC. *1979:* 19th WC; 17th EC. Was plagued by injury in 1982 when he lost ground. Czech ch since 1980.
One of the few competitors to have done a triple axel in a WC. Blond and very popular. Speaks fluent English.

Schramm, Norbert (FRG)
7.4.60, Oberstdorf. *T.* Erich Zeller
1983, 1982: 2nd WC; 1st EC. *1981:* 7th WC; 3rd EC. *1979:* 16th WC; 11th EC. West German ch 1981, 1979.
Known for his highly entertaining and unusual positions on the ice, such as a spin in which he puts his hands up and down while spinning at great speed, to create the impression of a speeded-up old film. Has enormous thigh muscles; it is this power which often keeps him upright on landing rather than a clean skating edge. In West German army.

Simond, Jean-Christophe (FRA)
29.4.60, Les Contamines.
T. Didier Gailhaguet
1983: 5th WC; 6th EC. *1982, 1981:* 5th WC; 2nd EC. *1980:* 13th WC; 7th OG. *1979:* 7th WC. *1977:* 15th WC.
Wanted to be skier but father killed in avalanche while skiing and mother would not let him. Stepfather was skating instructor. In last 3 WC won school figures but made mistakes in free skating.

WOMEN

Antonova, Anna (URS)
18.9.65, Leningrad. *T.* Alexei Mishin
1983: 7th EC. *1982:* 10th EC. 3rd in 1983
URS Ch.
*Known for extremely balletic style, but has
problems with jumping.*

Cariboni, Sandra (SWI)
17.11.63, Davos Platz *T.* Mother & Arnold
Gerschwiler
1983: 10th WC; 13th EC. *1982:* 16th WC;
13th EC. Swiss ch.
*Noted for her excellent school figures, but a
relatively poor free skater.*

Chin, Tiffany (USA)
10.3.67, Toluca Lake, Ca. *T.* John Nicks
1983: 9th WC on 1st appearance; 1st St Ivel;
3rd US Ch. *1981:* World Junior ch.
*Has a 'soft knee' which gives a very flowing
quality to her skating. Has done triple axel in
practice but not yet in competition.*

Dubravcic, Sanda (YUG)
24.8.64, Zagreb. *T.* Romana Gacnik
1983: 13th WC; 10th EC. *1981:* 2nd EC, but
has not been able to recapture that form. Has
competed in EC since 1977, and WC since
1979, with a highest place of 11th in 1981.
Yugoslav ch since 1976.
*Used to be known for her triple jumps, which
failed her as she got older.*

Jackson, Susan (GRB)
30.1.65, Nottingham. *T.* Arnold Gerschwiler
1983: 19th WC; 20th EC on 1st appearances.
1982: 3rd British Ch, but chosen for EC and
WC over 2nd-placed skater.
*Noted for free skating but held back by poor
school figures.*

Koch, Simone (GDR)
25.10.68, Dresden. *T.* Ingrid Lehmann
1983: 1st WJC, and will explode upon the
senior scene soon.
*A spectacular jumper, with clean, high triple
jumps in combination.*

Kondrashova, Anna (URS)
30.6.65, Moscow. *T.* Eduard Pliner
1983: 5th WC; 5th EC on 1st appearances;
2nd to Vodorezova URS Ch.
A very promising debut in international events.

Leistner, Claudia (FRG)
15.4.65, Ludwigshafen. *T.* Gunter Zoeller
1983: 2nd WC; 3rd EC. *1982:* 4th WC;
5th EC on 1st appearances.

*She is a spectacular jumper, though considered
lacking in artistic style. In 1983 she accomplished
by far the hardest combination of jumps in the
short programme section, a double toe loop to
triple toe loop.*

Ruben, Manuela 'Manoo' (FRG)
14.1.64, Frankfurt. *T.* Erich Zeller
1983: 8th WC; 4th EC. *1982:* 15th WC;
13th EC; 1st St Gervais Grand Prix;
1st Nebelhorn Trophy. *1981:* 13th WC;
10th EC. West German ch 1983, 1982. *1979:*
2nd WJC.
A former top-level competitive roller-skater.

Sumners, Rosalynn 'Roz' (USA)
20.4.64, Edmonds, Wa. *T.* Lorraine Borman
1983: 1st WC; 1st US Ch. *1982:* 6th WC;
1st US Ch; 1st Skate America. First took the
public eye in winning 1980 WJC, but skated
1982 with a hip injury.
*Noted for her artistic skating and polished
'feminine' style. Her highlight is an Ina Bauer
spread to an extremely high double axel. Hopes
to be an actress and has the physical attributes to
succeed – blonde hair, green eyes, 7 stone, 5' 2½''.*

Thomson, Kay (CAN)
18.2.64, Toronto. *T.* Louis Stong
1983: 7th WC. *1982:* 8th WC;
1st Moscow Skates. Canadian ch.
*Skated badly in the short programme in 1983
WC. Although her jumps do not have great
height, she is one of the few women to have
landed a triple lutz in competition. She is
undoubtedly the fastest woman spinner and does
spins in many unique positions. Her stylist is
Sandra Bezic.*

Vodorezova, Elena (URS)
21.5.63, Moscow.
1983: 3rd WC; 2nd EC, the highest a Russian
woman has ever been placed in singles. *1982:*
5th WC; 3rd EC. First took the public eye as a
spectacular free skater when, as a 12-year-old,
she was 11th in 1976 WC. *1978:* 3rd EC, but
then disappeared from the scene suffering
from arthritis in the knee. Reappeared in 1980
but did not complete EC and did not compete
internationally in 1981.
*Although free skating is not as spectacular as
when she was a child, her double axels are
highest of any woman competitor. Noted for her
excellent school figures. Rarely seen smiling.*

Wirth, Janina (GDR)
20.12.66, Berlin. *T.* Inge Wischnewski
1983: 11th WC; 8th EC. *1982:* 12th WC;
9th EC; 1st WJC.

Shows great potential for the future although still in the stage where she attempts more than she can bring off. Her trainer trained the 1974 World ch, Christine Errath.

Witt, Katarina (GDR)

3.12.65, Karl Marx Stadt.   *T.* Jutta Mueller
1983: 4th WC; 1st EC. *1982:* 2nd WC;
2nd EC. *1981:* 5th WC; 5th EC;
1st Ennia Cup. *1980:* 10th WC; 13th EC;
1st Vienna Cup. *1979:* 14th EC.
Known for her athletic style and array of triple jumps – and for the 'knickerbockers' in which she performed her short programme in 1983 EC. Her looks have been compared to those of top model and actress Brooke Shields. Her trainer also trained former world champions Gaby Seyfert, Anett Poetzsch and Jan Hoffmann.

Wong, Charlene (CAN)

4.3.66, Pierrefonds, Que.   *T.* Helen Shields
1983: 12th WC on 1st appearance; 2nd Canadian Ch. *1981:* 1st St Gervais Grand Prix.
A consistent skater though she is still developing her technique and her routine as yet lacks difficulty. Very pleasing style.

Wood, Karen (GRB)

15.7.62, Deeside.   *T.* Inge Dorn
1982: 17th WC; 8th EC. *1981:* 15th WC;
11th EC. British ch 1982, 1980. Withdrew from 1983 EC with illness after lying 18th at half-way stage, and was withdrawn from 1983 WC for disciplinary reasons.
Known for strong free skating and triple jumps performed at speed.

Zayak, Elaine (USA)

12.4.65, Paramus, NJ.   *T.* Peter Burrows
1982: 1st WC; 1st St Ivel. *1981:* 2nd WC;
1st US Ch. *1980:* 11th WC (4th in free after 22nd in schools); 1st Prague Skate. *1979:*
1st WJC. Had to withdraw from 1983 WC with stress fracture of right ankle.
When 2¼, part of left foot, from 2nd toe diagonally backwards, was lost in electric lawnmower. Took up skating on advice of doctors as means of making her use both legs equally. Left boot is specially stuffed to compensate. Known for her jumping ability, especially double lutz to triple toe loop combination. Her trainer is a former British pairs ch who has lived in US for many years.

Tiffany Chin (*below*) and Susan Jackson

Claudia Leistner

Rosalynn Sumners

Left: Kay Thomson
Below: Elena Vodorezova

Katarina Witt
Elaine Zayak

Karen Wood

PAIRS

Avstrijskaya, Marina, and
Kvashnin, Yuri (URS)
22.6.67, *and* 24.11.64, Moscow.
1983: 5th EC. 1983, *1982:* 1st WJC.

Baess, Sabine, and
Thierbach, Tassilo (GDR)
15.3.61, *and* 21.5.56, Karl Marx Stadt.
T. Irene Salzmann
1983: 2nd WC; 1st EC. *1982:* 1st WC; 1st EC.
1981: 2nd WC. *1980:* 4th WC; 4th EC;
6th OG. First win was at pre-Olympic try-out
at Lake Placid 1979. 5th on 1st appearances in
1978 WC. Did not compete in 1981 EC due to
injury; lost world title in 1983 on very close
decision.
Known for their throw moves, especially the
throw triple toe loop originated by them. He is a
TV repairman.

**Carruthers, Caitlin 'Kitty', and
Peter** (USA)
30.5.61, *and* 22.7.59, Wilmington, Del.
T. Ron Ludington
1983: 4th WC. *1982:* 3rd WC. *1981:*
1st NHK Trophy. *1980:* 7th WC; 5th OG.
1979: 1st St Gervais Grand Prix;
1st Nebelhorn Trophy. US ch since 1981.
*Known for their lateral-twist lift and 'Hydrant'
lift, both of which they originated.*

**Coull, Cynthia, and
Rowsom, Mark** (CAN)
14.8.65, Greenfield Park, Que., *and* 15.4.59,
Waterloo, Ont.   *T.* Kerry Leitch
1983: 9th WC. Although he had extensive
pair experience with his previous partner, she
had never skated pairs until summer 1982.
Shortly after, they were 4th in Skate America
and 2nd in Canadian Ch. She is a strong
singles skater (3rd in 1983 Canadian Ch and
1st reserve for WC women's event).
*Because both are such strong individual skaters,
they are able to carry out side-by-side difficult
jumps such as triple toe loops.*

**Garland, Susie, and
Jenkins, Ian** (GRB)
30.4.66, *and* 18.5.62, Bristol.
T. Anne Crompton
1983: 13th WC; 8th EC. Teamed together in
summer 1981, after she had split up with
previous partner, Robert Daw, with whom
she had competed in 1980 OG. She has been
British ch 5 times and Jenkins twice.

**Lorenz, Birgit, and
Schubert, Knut** (GDR)
2.8.63, *and* 9.9.58, East Berlin.
T. Uwe Kagelmann
1983: 8th WC; 3rd EC; 1st St Ivel. *1982:* 7th
WC; 5th EC *1981:* 4th EC. *1980:* 1st Prague
Skate.
*Known for their spreadeagles combined with
jumps. He was 9th in 1974 EC with his sister.*

**Matousek, Katherine, and
Eisler, Lloyd 'Herbie'** (CAN)
20.4.64, New Westminster, BC, *and*
28.4.63, Hamilton, Ont.   *T.* Kerry Leitch
1983: 10th WC; 3rd Canadian Ch. *1982:*
2nd St Gervais Grand Prix; 2nd Nebelhorn
Trophy; 6th Skate America. Both competed
internationally with previous partners.

**Miller, Lea Ann, and
Fauver, Bill** (USA)
22.1.61, *and* 2.3.54, Wilmington, Del.

T. Ron Ludington
1983: 7th WC. *1982:* 8th WC. *1981:* 10th WC.
He was 12th at 1976 OG with previous
partner, Alice Cook.
*Noted for their balletic style, and for their face-
down death spiral and their 'bowl' spin, nearly
sitting on the ice clasping each other tightly.*

**Pershina, Veronika, and
Akbarov, Marat** (URS)
5.4.66, *and* 3.2.61, Moscow.
T. Irina Rodnina
1983: 5th WC; 4th EC. *1982:* 6th WC; 4th EC.
1981: 6th WC; 5th EC. *1980:* 6th WC. *1979:*
1st WJC.
*He is from Sverdlovsk and moved to Moscow to
train with her under Stanislav Zhuk. Noted for
their speed and flow over the ice.*

**Pestova, Marina, and
Leonovich, Stanislav** (URS)
20.12.63, *and* 2.8.58, Sverdlovsk, now
Moscow.
1983: 6th WC. *1982:* 2nd WC; 2nd EC. *1981:*
5th EC *1980:* 3rd WC; 3rd EC; 4th OG.
1979: 5th WC; 4th EC. *1978:* 7th WC;
7th EC. She had a foot operation after 1983
URS Ch and they missed the EC and did
badly in WC.
*When first appeared were one of the '1¼' pairs –
he a full-sized adult, she a tiny child. Unlike
another of Zhuk's pairs, Marina Cherkasova
and Sergei Shakrai, the 1980 World ch who
faded after she grew, they have survived, but the
outcry against '1¼' pairs was so intense that
skaters must now be at least 15.*

**Preussler, Babette, and
Torsten, Ohlow** (GDR)
28.9.68, *and* 14.10.63, Berlin.
T. Heide Marie Walther-Steiner
1983: 12th WC; 6th EC. *1982:* 3rd WJC,
which allowed them to take part in EC and
WC although she is under age.

**Underhill, Barbara, and
Martini, Paul** (CAN)
24.6.63, Oshawa, Ont., *and*
2.11.60, Woodbridge, Ont.   *T.* Louis Stong
1983: 3rd WC. *1982:* 4th WC;
1st NHK Trophy. *1981:* 7th WC;
1st Skate America; 1st Ennia Cup. *1980:*
11th WC; 9th OG; 1st St Ivel;
1st NHK Trophy. Canadian ch since 1979.
1978: 1st WJC.
*Known for their spectacular lifts like the inverted
table-top and regular table-top. Stylist is Sandra
Bezic. Trained in 1982 in Los Angeles with
John Nicks. Tipped to win 1984 WC.*

Valova, Elena, and
Vasiliev, Oleg (URS)
4.1.63, *and* 22.11.59, Leningrad.
T. Tamara Moskvina
1983: 1st WC on 1st appearance; 2nd EC.
1982: 1st Skate America.
Won world title on 1st attempt, a feat previously
accomplished by Irina Rodnina and Alexei
Ulanov in 1969. Noted for their side-by-side
triple toe loops and their unusual choreography.

Watson, Jill, and
Lancon, Burt (USA)
29.3.63, Bloomington, Ind., *and*
13.11.60, Costa Mesa, Ca.   *T.* John Nicks
1983: 11th WC; 3rd US Ch.
Paired together in summer 1982.

Left: Sabine Baess & Tassilo Thierbach
Bottom left: Caitlin & Peter Carruthers
Bottom right: Lea Ann Miller & Bill Fauver
Below: Susie Garland & Ian Jenkins

Right: Marina Pestova & Stanislav Leonovich
Bottom right: Barbara Underhill &
Paul Martini
Bottom left: Elena Valova & Oleg Vasiliev
Below: Veronika Pershina & Marat Akbarov

ICE DANCE

Barber, Karen, and
Slater, Nicky (GRB)
21.6.61, *and* 6.4.58, Richmond.
T. Jimmy Young
1983: 5th WC; 3rd EC; 1st St Ivel. *1982:* 7th
WC; 5th EC; 1st Ennia Cup. *1981:* 7th WC;
5th EC; 1st Morzine Cup; 1st NHK Trophy.
1980: 10th WC; 8th EC; 12th OG. *1979:*
13th WC; 11th EC. Runners-up to Torvill
and Dean in British Ch since 1978.
Noted for their skills in the compulsories, in
which they make difficult moves look extremely
simple.

Batanova, Elena, and
Soloviev, Alexei (URS)
24.7.64, *and* 13.2.64, Moscow
T. Ludmila Pakhomova
1983: 8th WC. *1982:* 1st NHK Trophy.
1981, 1980: 1st WJC.
Trained by the winner of 1st OG gold medal in
ice dancing in 1976.

Bestemianova, Natalia, and
Bukin, Andrei (URS)
6.1.60, *and* 10.6.57, Moscow.
T. Tatiana Tarasova
1983: 2nd WC; 1st EC. *1982:* 2nd WC;
2nd EC. *1981:* 3rd WC; 4th EC. *1980:* 6th EC;
8th OG. *1979:* 10th WC.
Noted for the outgoing personality of the
beautiful red-haired Bestemianova and their
energetic style. The 'Charlie Chaplin' section of
their free dance was very well received on their
1st appearance in WC in 1979.

Blumberg, Judy, and
Seibert, Michael (USA)
13.9.57, Santa Monica, Ca. *and*
1.1.60, Eashington, Pa. *T.* Bobby Thompson
1983: 3rd WC. *1982, 1981:* 4th WC. *1980:*
6th WC; 7th OG. US ch since 1981. In 1983
WC were 2nd at halfway, but their 'Ginger
Rodgers and Fred Astaire' free dance was
judged marginally not difficult enough,
although it evoked the feeling of that era
extremely successfully.
Known for their steep edges in the compulsories
and for their speed, which has brought them to
grief (they fell badly in 1981 WC). Both had
previous partners at junior level; former British
world ch Doreen Denny suggested they team
together, but they only gelled at 2nd attempt.
Now trained by a Briton, skating wherever they
can get ice.

Born, Petra, and
Schonborn, Rainer (FRG)
1.8.65, *and* 26.5.62, Zweibrücken.
T. Martin Skotnicky
1983: 9th WC; 6th EC. *1982:* 14th WC;
11th EC. *1981:* 21st WC; 16th EC. West
German ch.
Train with Torvill and Dean at Oberstdorf and
have been helped with their compulsories by
Betty Callaway.

Fox, Carol, and
Dalley, Richard 'Beanie' (USA)
7.11.65, Westland, Mi., *and* 2.8.57, Lathrop
Village, Mi.   *T.* Ron Ludington
1982: 5th WC. *1981:* 1st Skate Canada;
1st Ennia Cup. He broke leg while skating in
Sept 1982 and in 1983 US Ch they were just
pipped for 2nd place, and USA could only
send 2 couples to 1983 WC, but will have 3 at
1984 WC and OG.

Herve, Nathalie, and
Bechu, Pierre (FRA)
28.3.63, Boulogne, *and* 10.3.59,
Viry-Chatillon.   *T.* Danièle Marotel
1983: 5th EC. French ch since 1979. Had to
withdraw from 1983 WC when lying 9th after
compulsories, due to his illness.

Hola, Jindra, and
Foltan, Karol (CSR)
2.10.60, *and* 16.4.59, Prague.
T. Vladimir Sobotka
1983: 9th EC. *1982:* 12th EC. *1981:* 13th EC.
1980: 14th WC. *1979:* 17th WC; 14th EC.
Czech ch. Missed 1983 WC because of her
illness.

Johnson, Kelly, and
Thomas, John (CAN)
27.9.61, Willowdale, Ont., *and*
5.9.60, Brampton, Ont.   *T.* Marijane Stong
1983: 10th WC on 1st appearance, only 3rd
international event. Partnership formed in
spring 1982.

Klimova, Marina, and
Ponomarenko, Sergei (URS)
28.7.66, *and* 6.10.60, Moscow.
T. Natalia Dubova
1983: 4th EC on 1st appearance. *1982:*
1st St Gervais Grand Prix;
1st Nebelhorn Trophy. He won 1978 and
1979 WJC with previous partner.
Betty Callaway thought they had the best
compulsories of all 3 Russian couples in EC.

Micheli, Isabella, and
Pelizzola, Roberto (ITA)
30.3.62, *and* 13.10.58, Milan
T. Paola Mezzardi and Joan Slater
1983: 11th WC; 8th EC. Italian ch.

Peterfy, Judit, and
Balint, Csaba (HUN)
8.9.64, *and* 13. 5.63, Budapest.
T. Ilona Berecz-Vedres
1983: 13th WC; 10th EC. *1982:* 8th EC. *1981:*
14th WC; 10th EC. *1980:* 2nd WJC.
Hungarian ch since 1982. Withdrew from
1982 WC because of illness.

Sato, Norika, and
Takahashi, Tadayu (JPN)
26.5.59, *and* 1.3.56, Tokyo.
T. Bobby Thompson and Yutaka Higuchi
1983: 14th WC. *1982:* 15th WC. *1981:*
16th WC. *1980:* 15th WC. Japanese ch since
1979.

Sessions, Wendy, and
Williams, Stephen (GRB)
3.1.59, *and* 23.5.60, Birmingham.   *T.* Bobby
Thompson, Gladys Hogg and Anne Crompton
1983: 12th WC; 7th EC. *1982:* 13th WC;
9th EC. *1981:* 11th WC; 9th EC. *1980:*
1st Nebelhorn Trophy. 3rd British Ch since
1980.

Spitz, Elisa 'Lisa', and
Gregory, Scott (USA)
17.5.63, *and* 31.7.59, Wilmington, Del.
T. Ron Ludington
1983: 7th WC; 2nd US Ch. *1982:* 8th WC;
1st Skate America; 1st Skate Canada.
Known for the energy they project on the ice.

Torvill, Jayne, and
Dean, Christopher (GRB)
7.10.57, *and* 27.7.58, Nottingham.
T. Betty Callaway
1983: 1st WC. *1982, 1981:* 1st WC; 1st EC.
1980: 4th WC; 4th EC; 5th OG. *1979:*
9th WC; 7th EC. *1978:* 11th WC; 9th EC.
1976: 1st St Gervais Grand Prix. Missed 1983
EC becase of her injury. Unbeaten anywhere
since 1980. British ch since 1978. In 1982 set
new records for the number of 6s awarded in
EC and WC and surpassed this in 1983 WC
with 7 6s in OSP and 9 in 2nd category of free
dance.

van Bommel, Marianne, and
Deweyert, Wayne (NED)
10.6.60, Belmont, Ont., *and* 1.12.59, London,
Ont.   *T.* Don Cumming
1983: 15th WC; 12th EC. *1982:* 16th WC;

15th EC. *1981:* 21st WC. Dutch ch. Live and
train in Canada.

Volozhinskaya, Olga, and
Svinin, Alexander (URS)
18.5.62, *and* 7.7.58, Moscow.
T. Elena Tchaikovskaya
1983: 4th WC; 2nd EC. *1982:* 6th WC;
4th EC. *1981:* 5th WC on 1st appearance.
*She is tall and very thin and uses her body very
flexibly.*

Wilson, Tracy, and
McCall, Bob (CAN)
25.9.61, Port Moody, BC, *and* 14.9.58,
Dartmouth, Nova Scotia.   *T.* Bernard Ford
1983: 6th WC. *1982:* 10th WC. Canadian ch
since 1982. He was Canadian ch previously
with former partner.
*Known for their very interpretive skating. Their
Rock and Roll OSP in 1983 WC very popular.
Trainer is former British world ch, now living in
Toronto.*

Karen Barber & Nicky Slater

Elena Batanova & Alexei Soloviev
Judy Blumberg & Michael Seibert

Natalia Bestemianova & Andrei Bukin

Carol Fox & Richard Dalley

Kelly Johnson & John Thomas

Wendy Sessions & Stephen Williams

Elisa Spitz & Scott Gregory   Tracy Wilson & Bob McCall
         Olga Volozhinskaya & Alexander Svinin

World Championship Medal Winners

There was no separate championship for women until 1906. A British woman, Mrs Madge Syers-Cave, entered the Championship in 1902, and since there was nothing in rules to forbid it, the ISU could not prevent her participation. However, the rules were immediately altered at the next meeting of the ISU to bar women from taking part.

In the early years of this century both the Women's and Pairs Championship (which started in 1908) were sometimes held separately from the men's event – in such cases, the different location is indicated.

Ice Dance was not included in the Championships until 1952.

Note: before 1945 Germany is given as GER; before 1914 Russia as RUS. The results of each year's Championship are listed in the following order: Men's Singles, Women's Singles, Pairs, Ice Dance

1896 St Petersburg
Gilbert Fuchs (GER)
Gustav Hügel (AUT)
Georg Sanders (RUS)

1897 Stockholm
Hügel (AUT)
Ulrich Salchow (SWE)
Johan Lefstad (NOR)

1898 London
Henning Grenander (SWE)
Hügel (AUT)
Fuchs (GER)

1899 Davos
Hügel (AUT)
Salchow (SWE)
Edgar Syers (GRB)

1900 Davos
Hügel (AUT)
Salchow (SWE)
(only 2 entrants)

1901 Stockholm
Salchow (SWE)
Fuchs (GER)
(only 2 entrants)

1902 London
Salchow (SWE)
Mrs Madge Syers-Cave (GRB)
Martin Gordan (GER)

1903 St Petersburg
Salchow (SWE)

Nicolai Panin (RUS)
Max Bohatsch (AUT)

1904 Berlin
Salchow (SWE)
Heinrich Burger (Ger)
Gordan (FRG)

1905 Stockholm
Salchow (SWE)
Bohatsch (AUT)
Per Thoren (SWE)

1906 Munich/Davos (Women's)
Fuchs (GER)
Burger (GER)
Bror Meyer (SWE)

Madge Syers-Cave (GRB)
Jenny Herz (AUT)
Lily Kronberger (HUN)

1907 Vienna
Salchow (SWE)
Bohatsch (AUT)
Fuchs (GER)

Syers-Cave (GRB)
Herz (AUT)
Kronberger (HUN)

1908 Troppau/S Petersburg (Pairs)
Salchow (SWE)
Fuchs (GER)
Burger (GER)

Kronberger (HUN)
Elsa Rendschmidt (GER)
(only 2 entrants)

Anna Hubler & Heinrich Burger (GER)
Phyllis & James Johnson (GRB)
A. L. Fischer & L. P. Popowa (RUS)

1909 Stockholm/Budapest (Women's)
Salchow (SWE)
Thoren (SWE)
Ernest Herz (AUT)

Kronberger (HUN)
(only 1 entrant)

Johnson & Johnson (GRB)
Valborg Lindahl & Nils Rosenius (SWE)
Gertrud Strom & Richard Johanson (SWE)

1910 Davos/Berlin (Women's & Pairs)
Salchow (SWE)
Werner Rittberger (GER)
Andor Szende (HUN)

Kronberger (HUN)
Rendschmidt (GER)
(only 2 entrants)

Hubler & Burger (GER)
Ludowika Eilers & Walter Jakobsson
(GER/FIN)
Johnson & Johnson (GRB)

1911 Berlin/Vienna (Women's & Pairs)
Salchow (SWE)
Rittberger (FRG)
Fritz Kachler (AUT)

Kronberger (HUN)
Opika von Meray Horvath (HUN)
Ludowika Eilers (GER)

Eilers & Jakobsson (GER/FIN)
(only 1 pair entered)

1912 Manchester/Davos (Women's)
Kachler (AUT)
Rittberger (GER)
Szende (HUN)

von Meray Horvath (HUN)
Dorothy Greenhough-Smith (GRB)
Phyllis Johnson (GRB)

Johnson & Johnson (GRB)
Eilers & Jakobsson (GER/FIN)
Alexia Schoyen & Yngvar Bryn (NOR)

1913 Vienna/Stockholm (Women's & Pairs)
Kachler (AUT)
Willy Bröckl (AUT)
Szende (HUN)

von Meray Horvath (HUN)
Johnson (GRB)
Svea Noren (SWE)

Helene Engelmann & Karl Mejstrik (AUT)
Eilers & Jakobsson (FIN)
Christa von Szabo & Leo Horwitz (AUT)

1914 Helsinki/St Moritz (Women's & Pairs)
Gosta Sandahl (SWE)
Kachler (AUT)
Bröckl (AUT)

von Meray Horvath (HUN)
Angela Hanka (AUT)
Johnson (GRB)

Eilers & Jakobsson (FIN)
Engelmann & Mejstrik (AUT)
von Szabo & Horwitz (AUT)

*No World Championships were held between
1915 and 1921 because of the First World War*

1922 Stockholm/Davos (Pairs)
Gillis Grafstrom (SWE)
Kachler (AUT)
Bröckl (AUT)

Herma Plank-Szabo (AUT)
Noren (SWE)
Margot Moe (NOR)

Engelmann & Alfred Berger (AUT)
Eilers & Jakobsson (FIN)
Margaret & Paul Metzner (GER)

1923 Vienna/Oslo (Pairs)
Kachler (AUT)
Bröckl (AUT)
Sandahl (SWE)

Plank-Szabo (AUT)
Gisela Reichmann (AUT)
Noren (SWE)

Eilers & Jakobsson (FIN)
Schoyen & Bryn (NOR)
Eina Henrikson & Kaj af Ekstrom (SWE)

1924 Manchester/Oslo (Women's)
Grafstrom (SWE)
Bröckl (AUT)
Ernst Oppacher (AUT)

Herma Jaross-Szabo (AUT)
Ellen Brockhofft (GER)
Noren (SWE)

Engelmann & Berger (AUT)
Ethel Muckelt & John Page (GRB)
Henrikson & af Ekstrom (SWE)

1925 Vienna/Davos (Women's)
Bröckl (AUT)
Kachler (AUT)
Otto Preissecker (AUT)

Jaross-Szabo (AUT)
Brockhofft (GER)
Elisabeth Bockel (GER)

Jaross-Szabo & Ludwig Wrede (AUT)
Andrée Joly & Pierre Brunet (FRA)
Lilly Scholz & Otto Kaiser (AUT)

1926 Berlin/Stockholm (Women's)
Bröckl (AUT)
Preissecker (AUT)
John Page (GRB)

Jaross-Szabo (AUT)
Sonja Henie (NOR)
Kathleen Shaw (GRB)

Joly & Brunet (FRA)
Scholz & Kaiser (AUT)
Jaross-Szabo & Wrede (AUT)

1927 Davos/Oslo (Women's)/Vienna (Pairs)
Bröckl (AUT)
Preissecker (AUT)
Karl Schäfer (AUT)

Henie (NOR)
Jaross-Szabo (AUT)
Karen Simensen (NOR)

Jaross-Szabo & Wrede (AUT)
Scholz & Kaiser (AUT)
Else & Oscar Hoppe (CSR)

1928 Berlin/London (Women's & Pairs)
Bröckl (AUT)
Schäfer (AUT)
Hugo Distler (AUT)

Henie (NOR)
Maribel Vinson (USA)
Fritzi Burger (AUT)

Joly & Brunet (FRA)
Scholz & Kaiser (AUT)
Melitta Brunner & Wrede (AUT)

1929 London/Budapest (Women's & Pairs)
Grafstrom (SWE)
Schäfer (AUT)
Ludwig Wrede (AUT)

Henie (NOR)
Burger (AUT)
Melitta Brunner (AUT)

Scholz & Kaiser (AUT)
Brunner & Wrede (AUT)
Olga Orgonista & Sandor Szalay (HUN)

1930 New York
Schäfer (AUT)
Roger Turner (USA)
Georg Gautschi (SWI)

Henie (NOR)
Cecil Smith (CAN)
Vinson (USA)

Joly & Brunet (FRA)
Brunner & Wrede (AUT)
Beatrix Loughran & Sherwin Badger (USA)

1931 Berlin
Schäfer (AUT)
Turner (USA)
Ernst Baier (GER)

Henie (NOR)
Hilde Holovsky (AUT)
Burger (AUT)

Emile Rotter & Laszlo Szollas (HUN)
Orgonista & Szalay (HUN)
Ida Papez & Karl Zwack (AUT)

1932 Montreal
Schäfer (AUT)
Montgomery Wilson (CAN)
Baier (GER)

Henie (NOR)
Burger (AUT)
Constance Samuel (CAN)

Joly & Brunet (FRA)
Rotter & Szollas (HUN)
Loughran & Badger (USA)

1933 Zurich/Stockholm (Women's & Pairs)
Schäfer (AUT)
Baier (GER)
Markus Nikkanen (FIN)

Henie (NOR)
Vivi-Anne Hulten (SWE)
Holovsky (AUT)

Rotter & Szollas (HUN)
Papez & Zwack (AUT)
Randi Bakke & Christen Christensen (NOR)

1934 Stockholm/Oslo (Women's) Helsinki (Pairs)
Schäfer (AUT)
Baier (GER)
Erich Erdos (AUT)

Henie (NOR)
Megan Taylor (GRB)
Liselotte Landbeck (AUT)

Rotter & Szollas (HUN)
Papez & Zwack (AUT)
Maxi Herber & Ernst Baier (GER)

1935 Budapest/Vienna (Women's)
Schäfer (AUT)
Jack Dunn (GRB)

Denes Pataky (HUN)

Henie (NOR)
Cecilia Colledge (GRB)
Hulten (SWE)

Rotter & Szollas (HUN)
Ilse & Erich Pausin (AUT)
Lucy Gallo & Rezso Dillinger (HUN)

1936 Paris
Schäfer (AUT)
Graham Sharp (GRB)
Felix Kaspar (AUT)

Henie (NOR)
Taylor (GRB)
Hulten (SWE)

Herber & Baier (GER)
Pausin & Pausin (AUT)
Violet & Leslie Cliff (GRB)

1937 Vienna/London (Women's & Pairs)
Kaspar (AUT)
Sharp (GRB)
Elmer Tertak (HUN)

Colledge (GRB)
Taylor (GRB)
Hulten (SWE)

Herber & Baier (GER)
Pausin & Pausin (AUT)
Cliff & Cliff (GRB)

1938 Berlin/Stockholm (Women's)
Kaspar (AUT)
Sharp (GRB)
Herbert Alward (AUT)

Taylor (GRB)
Colledge (GRB)
Hedy Stenuf (USA)

Herber & Baier (GER)
Pausin & Pausin (AUT)
Inge Koch & Gunther Noack (GER)

1939 Budapest/Prague (Women's)
Sharp (GRB)
Frederick Tomlins (GRB)
Horst Faber (GER)

Taylor (GRB)
Stenuf (USA)
Daphne Walker (GRB)

Herber & Baier (GER)
Pausin & Pausin (AUT)
Koch & Noack (GER)

No World Championships were held between 1940 and 1946 because of the Second World War

1947 Stockholm
Hans Gerschwiler (SWI)
Richard Button (USA)
Arthur Apfel (GRB)

Barbara Ann Scott (CAN)
Daphne Walker (GRB)
Gretchen Merill (USA)

Micheline Lannoy & Pierre Baugniet (BEL)
Karol & Peter Kennedy (USA)
Suzanne Diskeuve & Edmond Verbustel (BEL)

1948 Davos
Button (USA)
Gerschwiler (SWI)
Ede Kiraly (HUN)

Scott (CAN)
Eva Pawlik (AUT)
Jirina Nekolova (CSR)

Lannoy & Baugniet (BEL)
Andrea Kékesy & Ede Kiraly (HUN)
Suzanne Morrow & Wallace Distelmeyer (CAN)

1949 Paris
Button (USA)
Kiraly (HUN)
Edi Rada (AUT)

Alena Vrzanova (CSR)
Yvonne Sherman (USA)
Jeannette Altwegg (GRB)

Kékesy & Kiraly (HUN)
Kennedy & Kennedy (USA)
Ann Davies & Carleton Hoffner (USA)

1950 London
Button (USA)
Kiraly (HUN)
Hayes Alan Jenkins (USA)

Vrzanova (CSR)
Altwegg (GRB)
Sherman (USA)

Kennedy & Kennedy (USA)
Jennifer & John Nicks (GRB)
Marianne & Laszlo Nagy (HUN)

1951 Milan
Button (USA)
James Grogan (USA)
Helmut Seibt (AUT)

Altwegg (GRB)
Jacqueline du Bief (FRA)
Sonja Klopfer (USA)

Ria Baran & Paul Falk (FRG)
Kennedy & Kennedy (USA)
Nicks & Nicks (GRB)

1952 Paris
Button (USA)
Grogan (USA)
Jenkins (USA)

du Bief (FRA)
Klopfer (USA)
Virginia Baxter (USA)

Ria & Paul Falk (FGR)
Kennedy & Kennedy (USA)
Nicks & Nicks (GRB)

Jean Westwood & Lawrence Demmy (GRB)
Joan Dewhirst & John Slater (GRB)
Carol Peters & Daniel Ryan (USA)

1953 Davos
Jenkins (USA)
Grogan (USA)
Carlo Fassi (ITA)

Tenley Albright (USA)
Gundi Busch (FRG)
Valda Osborn (GRB)

Nicks & Nicks (GRB)
Frances Dafoe & Norris Bowden (CAN)
Nagy & Nagy (HUN)

Westwood & Demmy (GRB)
Dewhirst & Slater (GRB)
Peters & Ryan (USA)

1954 Oslo
Jenkins (USA)
Grogan (USA)
Alain Giletti (FRA)

Busch (FRG)
Albright (USA)
Erica Batchelor (GRB)

Dafoe & Bowden (CAN)
Silvia & Michel Grandjean (SWI)
Sissy Schwarz & Kurt Oppelt (AUT)

Westwood & Demmy (GRB)
Nesta Davies & Paul Thomas (GRB)
Carmel & Edward Bodel (USA)

1955 Vienna
Jenkins (USA)
Ronald Robertson (USA)
David Jenkins (USA)

Albright (USA)
Carol Heiss (USA)
Hanna Eigel (AUT)

Dafoe & Bowden (CAN)
Schwarz & Oppelt (AUT)
Nagy & Nagy (HUN)

Westwood & Demmy (GRB)
Pamela Weight & Thomas (GRB)
Barbara Radford & Raymond Lockwood (GRB)

1956 Garmisch-Partenkirchen
Jenkins (USA)
Robertson (USA)
D. Jenkins (USA)

Heiss (USA)
Albright (USA)
Ingrid Wendl (AUT)

Schwarz & Oppelt (AUT)
Dafoe & Bowden (CAN)
Marika Kilius & Franz Ningel (FRG)

Weight & Thomas (GRB)
June Markham & Courtney Jones (GRB)
Barbara Thompson & Gerard Rigby (GRB)

1957 Colorado Springs
D. Jenkins (USA)
Tim Brown (USA)
Charles Snelling (CAN)

Heiss (USA)
Eigel (AUT)
Wendl (AUT)

Barbara Wagner & Robert Paul (CAN)
Kilius & Ningel (FRG)
Maria & Otto Jelinek (CAN)

Markham & Jones (GRB)
Geraldine Fenton & William McLachlan
(CAN)
Sharon McKenzie & Bert Wright (USA)

1958 Paris
D. Jenkins (USA)
Brown (USA)
Giletti (FRA)

Heiss (USA)
Wendl (AUT)
Hanna Walter (AUT)

Wagner & Paul (CAN)
Vera Suchankova & Zdenek Dolezal (CSR)
Jelinek & Jelinek (CAN)

Markham & Jones (GRB)
Fenton & McLachlan (CAN)
Andree Anderson & Donald Jacoby (USA)

1959 Colorado Springs
D. Jenkins (USA)
Donald Jackson (CAN)
Brown (USA)

Heiss (USA)
Walter (AUT)
Sjoukje Dijkstra (NED)

Wagner & Paul (CAN)
Kilius & Hans Jurgen Baumler (FRG)
Nancy & Ronald Ludington (USA)

Doreen Denny & Jones (GRB)
Anderson & Jacoby (USA)
Fenton & McLachan (CAN)

1960 Vancouver
Giletti (FRA)
Jackson (CAN)
Alain Calmat (FRA)

Heiss (USA)
Dijkstra (NED)
Barbara Roles (USA)

Wagner & Paul (CAN)
Jelinek & Jelinek (CAN)
Kilius & Baumler (FRG)

Denny & Jones (GRB)
Virginia Thompson & McLachan (CAN)
Christiane & Jean Paul Guhel (FRA)

The 1961 World Championships, due to take place in Prague, were cancelled because of the Brussels air disaster in which the entire US team, on its way to the event, were killed.

1962 Prague
Jackson (CAN)
Karol Divin (CSR)
Calmat (FRA)

Dijkstra (NED)
Wendy Griner (CAN)
Regine Heitzer (AUT)

Jelinek & Jelinek (CAN)
Ludmila Belousova & Oleg Protopopov (URS)
Margaret Gobl & Franz Nigel (FRG)

Eva & Pavel Roman (CSR)
Guhel & Guhel (FRA)
Thompson & McLachlan (CAN)

1963 Cortina d'Ampezzo
Donald McPherson (CAN)
Calmat (FRA)
Manfred Schnelldorfer (FRG)

Dijkstra (NED)
Heitzer (AUT)
Nicole Hassler (FRA)

Kilius & Baumler (FRG)
Belousova & Protopopov (URS)
Tatiana Zhuk & Alexander Gorelik (URS)

Roman & Roman (CSR)
Linda Shearman & Michael Phillips (GRB)
Paulette Doan & Kenneth Ormsby (CAN)

1964 Dortmund
Schnelldorfer (FRG)
Calmat (FRA)
Divin (CSR)

Dijkstra (NED)
Heitzer (AUT)
Petra Burka (CAN)

Kilius & Baumler (FRG)
Belousova & Protopopov (URS)
Debbie Wilkes & Guy Revell (CAN)

Roman & Roman (CSR)
Doan & Ormsby (CAN)
Janet Sawbridge & David Hickinbottom (GRB)

1965 Colorado Springs
Calmat (FRA)
Scott Allen (USA)
Donald Knight (CAN)

Burka (CAN)
Heitzer (AUT)
Peggy Fleming (USA)

Belousova & Protopopov (URS)
Vivian & Ronald Joseph (USA)
Zhuk & Gorelik (URS)

Roman & Roman (CSR)
Sawbridge & Hickinbottom (GRB)
Lorna Dyer & John Carrell (USA)

1966 Davos
Emmerich Danzer (AUT)
Wolfgang Schwarz (AUT)
Gary Visconti (USA)

Fleming (USA)
Gaby Seyfert (GDR)
Burka (CAN)

Ludmila & Oleg Protopopov (URS)
Zhuk & Gorelik (URS)
Cynthia & Ron Kauffmann (USA)

Diane Towler & Bernard Ford (GRB)
Kristin Fortune & Dennis Sveum (USA)
Dyer & Carrell (USA)

1967 Vienna
Danzer (AUT)
Schwarz (AUT)
Visconti (USA)

Fleming (USA)
Seyfert (GDR)
Hana Maskova (CSR)

Protopopov & Protopopov (URS)
Margot Glockshuber & Wolfgang Danne (FRG)
Kauffman & Kauffman (USA)

Towler & Ford (GRB)
Dyer & Carrell (USA)
Yvonne Suddick & Malcolm Cannon (GRB)

1968 Geneva
Danzer (AUT)
Tim Wood (USA)
Patrick Pera (FRA)

Fleming (USA)
Seyfert (GDR)
Maskova (CSR)

Protopopov & Protopopov (URS)
Zhuk & Gorelik (URS)
Kauffman & Kauffman (USA)

Towler & Ford (GRB)
Suddick & Cannon (GRB)
Sawbridge & Jon Lane (GRB)

1969 Colorado Springs
Wood (USA)
Ondrej Nepela (CSR)
Pera (FRA)

Seyfert (GDR)
Beatrix Schuba (AUT)
Zsuzsa Almassy (HUN)

Irina Rodnina & Alexei Ulanov (URS)
Tamara Moskvina & Alexei Mishin (URS)
Protopopov & Protopopov (URS)

Towler & Ford (GRB)
Ludmila Pakhomova & Alexander Gorshkov
(URS)
Judy Schwomeyer & James Sladky (USA)

1970 Ljubljana
Wood (USA)
Nepela (CSR)
Gunter Zoller (GDR)

Seyfert (GDR)
Schuba (AUT)
Julie Holmes (USA)

Rodnina & Ulanov (URS)
Ludmila Smirnova & Andrei Suraikin (URS)
Heide Marie Steiner & Heinz Ulrich Walther
(GDR)

Pakhomova & Gorshkov (URS)
Schwomeyer & Sladky (USA)
Angelika & Erich Buck (FRG)

1971 Lyons
Nepela (CSR)
Pera (FRA)
Sergei Chetverukin (URS)

Schuba (AUT)
Holmes (USA)

Karen Magnussen (CAN)

Rodnina & Ulanov (URS)
Smirnova & Suraikin (URS)
Jo Jo Starbuck & Ken Shelley (USA)

Pakhomova & Gorshkov (URS)
Buck & Buck (FRG)
Schwomeyer & Sladky (USA)

1972 Calgary
Nepela (CSR)
Chetverukin (URS)
Vladimir Kovalev (URS)

Schuba (AUT)
Magnussen (CAN)
Janet Lynn (USA)

Rodnina & Ulanov (URS)
Smirnova & Suraikin (URS)
Starbuck & Shelley (USA)

Pakhomova & Gorshkov (URS)
Buck & Buck (FRG)
Schwomeyer & Sladky (USA)

1973 Bratislava
Nepela (CSR)
Chetverukin (URS)
Jan Hoffmann (GDR)

Magnussen (CAN)
Lynn (USA)
Christine Errath (GDR)

Rodnina & Alexander Zaitsev (URS)
Smirnova & Ulanov (URS)
Manuela Gross & Uwe Kagelmann (DGR)

Pakhomova & Gorshkov (URS)
Buck & Buck (FRG)
Hilary Green & Glyn Watts (GRB)

1974 Munich
Hoffmann (GDR)
Sergei Volkov (URS)
Toller Cranston (CAN)

Errath (GDR)
Dorothy Hamill (USA)
Dianne de Leeuw (NED)

Rodnina & Zaitsev (URS)
Smirnova & Ulanov (URS)
Romy Kermer & Rolf Oesterreich (GDR)

Pakhomova & Gorshkov (URS)
Green & Watts (GRB)
Natalia Linichuk & Gennadi Karponosov (URS)

1975 Colorado Springs
Volkov (URS)
Kovalev (URS)

John Curry (GRB)

de Leeuw (NED)
Hamill (USA)
Errath (GDR)

Rodnina & Zaitsev (URS)
Kermer & Oesterreich (GDR)
Gross & Kagelmann (GDR)

Irina Moiseeva & Andrei Minenkov (URS)
Colleen O'Connor & Jim Millns (USA)
Green & Watts (GRB)

1976 Göteborg
Curry (GRB)
Kovalev (URS)
Hoffmann (GDR)

Hamill (USA)
Errath (GDR)
de Leeuw (NED)

Rodnina & Zaitsev (URS)
Kermer & Oesterreich (GDR)
Gross & Kagelmann (GDR)

Pakhomova & Gorshkov (URS)
Moiseeva & Minenkov (URS)
O'Connor & Millns (USA)

1977 Tokyo
Kovalev (URS)
Hoffmann (GDR)
Minoru Sano (JPN)

Linda Fratianne (USA)
Anett Poetzsch (GDR)
Dagmar Lurz (FRG)

Rodnina & Zaitsev (URS)
Irina Vorobieva & Alexander Vlasov (URS)
Tai Babilonia & Randy Gardner (USA)

Moiseeva & Minenkov (URS)
Janet Thompson & Warren Maxwell (GRB)
Linichuk & Karponosov (URS)

1978 Ottawa
Charles Tickner (USA)
Hoffmann (GDR)
Robin Cousins (GRB)

Poetzsch (GDR)
Fratianne (USA)
Susan Driano (ITA)

Rodnina & Zaitsev (URS)
Manuela Mager & Uwe Bewersdorf (GDR)
Babilonia & Gardner (USA)

Linichuk & Karponosov (URS)
Moiseeva & Minenkov (URS)
Kristina Regoeczy & Andras Sallay (HUN)

1979 Vienna
Kovalev (URS)
Cousins (GRB)
Hoffmann (GDR)

Fratianne (USA)
Poetzsch (GDR)
Emi Watanabe (JPN)

Babilonia & Gardner (USA)
Marina Cherkasova & Sergei Shakhrai (URS)
Sabine Baess & Tassilo Thierbach (GDR)

Linichuk & Karponosov (URS)
Regoeczy & Sallay (HUN)
Moiseeva & Minenkov (URS)

1980 Dortmund
Hoffmann (GDR)
Cousins (GRB)
Tickner (USA)

Poetzsch (GDR)
Lurz (FRG)
Fratianne (USA)

Cherkasova & Shakhrai (URS)
Mager & Bewersdorf (GDR)
Marina Pestova & Stanislav Leonovich (URS)

Regoeczy & Sallay (HUN)
Linichuk & Karponosov (URS)
Moiseeva & Minenkov (URS)

1981 Hartford
Scott Hamilton (USA)
David Santee (USA)
Igor Bobrin (URS)

Denise Biellmann (SWI)
Elaine Zayak (USA)
Claudia Kristofics-Binder (AUT)

Vorobieva & Igor Lisovsky (URS)
Baess & Thierbach (GDR)
Christina Riegel & Andreas Nischwitz (FRG)

Jayne Torvill & Christopher Dean (GRB)
Moiseeva & Minenkov (URS)
Natalia Bestemianova & Andrei Bukin (URS)

1982 Copenhagen
Hamilton (USA)
Norbert Schramm (FRG)
Brian Pocker (CAN)

Zayak (USA)
Katarina Witt (GDR)
Kristofics-Binder (AUT)

Baess & Thierbach (GDR)
Pestova & Leonovich (URS)
Kitty & Peter Carruthers (USA)

Torvill & Dean (GRB)
Bestemianova & Bukin (URS)
Moiseeva & Minenkov (URS)

1983 Helsinki
Hamilton (USA)
Schramm (FRG)
Brian Orser (CAN)

Rosalynn Sumners (USA)
Claudia Leistner (FRG)
Elena Vodorezova (URS)

Elena Valova & Oleg Vasiliev (URS)
Baess & Thierbach (GDR)
Barbara Underhill & Paul Martini (CAN)

Torvill & Dean (GRB)
Bestemianova & Bukin (URS)
Judy Blumberg & Michael Seibert (USA)

Olympic Medal Winners, plus British Placings

Skating was held as an event in the Olympic Games of 1908 and 1920. The first separate Winter Olympic Games were held in 1924 at Chamonix.
Results are listed in the following order: Men's Singles, Women's Singles, Pairs.

London 1908
Ulrich Salchow (SWE)
Richard Johansson (SWE)
Per Thoren (SWE)
4. John Keiller Greig (GRB)
5. A March (GRB)

Madge Syers-Cave (GRB)
Elsa Rendschmidt (GER)
Dorothy Greenhough-Smith (GRB)
5. Gwendolyn Lycett (GRB)

Anna Hubler & Heinrich Burger (GER)
Phyllis & James Johnson (GRB)
Madge & Edgar Syers Cave (GRB)
Special Figures:
Nicolai Panin (RUS)
Arthur Cumming (GRB)
George Hall-Say (GRB)

Antwerp 1920
Gillis Grafstrom (SWE)
Andreas Krogh (NOR)
Martin Stixrud (NOR)
7. Basil Williams (GRB)
9. Kenneth Macdonald Beaumont (GRB)

Magda Julin Mauroy (SWE)
Svea Noren (SWE)
Theresa Weld (USA)
4. Phyllis Johnson (GRB)

Ludowika Eilers & Walter Jakobsson (FIN)
Alexia Schoyen & Yngvar Bryn (NOR)
Phyllis Johnson & Basil Williams (GRB)
5. Ethel Muckelt & Sydney Wallwork (GRB)
8. Madeleine & Kenneth Macdonald
    Beaumont (GRB)

Chamonix 1924
Grafstrom (SWE)
Willy Bröckl (AUT)
Georg Gautschi (SWI)
5. John Page (GRB)
10. Herbert Clarke (GRB)

Herma Plank-Szabo (AUT)
Beatrix Loughran (USA)
Ethel Muckelt (GRB)
7. Kathleen Shaw (GRB)

Helene Englemann & Alfred Berger (AUT)
Ludowika Eilers & Walter Jakobsson (FIN)
Andrée Joly & Pierre Brunet (FRA)
4. Muckelt & John Page (GRB)
8. Mildred & Thomas Dow Richardson (GRB)

St Moritz 1928
Grafstrom (SWE)
Willy Bröckl (AUT)
Robert van Zeebroeck (BEL)
9. Page (GRB)
14. Ian Bowhill (GRB)

Sonja Henie (NOR)
Fritzi Burger (AUT)
Loughran (USA)
14. Shaw (GRB)

Joly & Brunet (FRA)
Lilly Scholz & Otto Kaiser (AUT)
Melitta Brunner & Ludwig Wrede (AUT)
7. Muckelt & Page (GRB)
13. Kathleen Lovett & Proktor Burman (GRB)

Lake Placid 1932
Karl Schäfer (AUT)
Grafstrom (SWE)
Montgomery Wilson (CAN)

Henie (NOR)
Burger (AUT)
Maribel Vinson (USA)
7. Megan Taylor (GRB)
8. Cecilia Colledge (GRB)
9. Mollie Phillips (GRB)
10. Joan Dix (GRB)

Joly & Brunet (FRA)
Beatrix Loughran & Sherwin Badger (USA)
Emilie Rotter & Laszlo Szollas (HUN)

Garmisch-Partenkirchen 1936
Schäfer (AUT)
Ernst Baier (GER)
Felix Kaspar (AUT)
5. Graham Sharp (GRB)
6. Jack Dunn (GRB)
10. Frederick Tomlins (GRB)
16. Geoffrey Yates (GRB)

Henie (NOR)
Colledge (GRB)
Vivi-Anne Hulten (SWE)
11. Phillips (GRB)
16. Belita Jepson-Turner (GRB)

Maxi Herber & Ernst Baier (GER)
Ilse & Erich Pausin (AUT)
Rotter & Szollas (HUN)
7. Violet & Leslie Cliff (GRB)
10 Rosemarie Stewart & Ernst Yates (GRB)

St Moritz 1948
Richard Button (USA)
Hans Gerschwiler (SWI)
Edi Rada (AUT)
7. Graham Sharp (GRB)

Barbara Ann Scott (CAN)
Eva Pawlik (AUT)
Jeannette Altwegg (GRB)
7. Bridget Adams (GRB)
10. Marion Davies (GRB)
19. Jill Hodd-Linzee (GRB)

Micheline Lannoy & Pierre Baugniet (BEL)
Andrea Kékesy & Ede Kiraly (HUN)
Suzanne Morrow & Wallace Distelmeyer
   (CAN)
5. Winifred & Dennis Silverthorne (GRB)
8. Jennifer & John Nicks (GRB)

Oslo 1952
Button (USA)
Helmut Seibt (AUT)
James Grogan (USA)

Altwegg (GRB)
Tenley Albright (USA)
Jacqueline de Bief (FRA)
7. Barbara Wyatt (GRB)
11. Valda Osborn (GRB)
17. Patricia Devries (GRB)

Ria Baran & Paul Falk (FRG)
Karol & Peter Kennedy (USA)
Marianne & Laszlo Nagy (HUN)
4. Nicks & Nicks (GRB)
11. Peri Horne & Raymond Lockwood (GRB)

Cortina D'Ampezzo 1956
Hayes Alan Jenkins (USA)
Ronald Robertson (USA)
David Jenkins (USA)
6. Michael Booker (GRB)

Tenley Albright (USA)
Carol Heiss (USA)
Ingrid Wendl (AUT)
4. Yvonne Sugden (GRB)
11. Erica Batchelor (GRB)
14. Dianne Peach (GRB)

Elisabeth Schwarz & Kurt Oppelt (AUT)
Frances Dafoe & Norris Bowden (CAN)
Nagy & Nagy (HUN)
10. Joyce Coates & Anthony Holles (GRB)
11. Carolyn Krau & Rodney Ward (GRB)

Squaw Valley 1960
Jenkins (USA)
Karol Divin (CSR)
Donald Jackson (CAN)
12. Robin Jones (GRB)
15. David Clements (GRB)

Carol Heiss (USA)
Sjoukje Dijkstra (NED)
Barbara Ann Roles (USA)
15. Patricia Pauley (GRB)
19. Carolyn Kray (GRB)

Barbara Wagner & Robert Paul (CAN)
Marika Kilius & Hans Jurgen Baumler (FRG)
Nancy & Ron Ludington (USA)

Innsbruck 1964
Manfred Schnelldorfer (FRG)
Alain Calmat (FRA)
Scott Allen (USA)
18. Hywel Evans (GRB)
20. Malcolm Cannon (GRB)

Sjoukje Dijkstra (NED)
Regine Heitzer (AUT)
Petra Burka (CAN)
11. Sally Stapleford (GRB)
16. Carol-Ann Warner (GRB)
18 Diana Clifton-Peach (GRB)

Ludmila Belousova & Oleg Protopopov (URS)
Marika Kilius & Hans Jurgen Baumler (FRG)
Debbie Wilkes & Guy Revell (CAN)

Grenoble 1968
Wolfgang Schwarz (AUT)
Tim Wood (USA)
Patrick Pera (FRA)
15. Michael Williams (GRB)
17. Haig Oundjian (GRB)

Peggy Fleming (USA)
Gaby Seyfert (GDR)
Hana Maskova (CSR)
11. Stapleford (GRB)
15. Pat Dodd (GRB)

Ludmila & Oleg Protopopov (URS)
Tatiana Zhuk & Alexander Gorelik (URS)
Margot Glockshuber & Wolfgang Danne (FRG)
18. Linda Bernard & Raymond Wilson (GRB)

Sapporo 1972
Ondrej Nepela (CSR)
Sergei Chetverukin (URS)
Pera (FRA)
7. Oundjian (GRB)
11. John Curry (GRB)

Beatrix Schuba (AUT)
Karen Magnussen (CAN)
Janet Lynn (USA)
11. Jean Scott (GRB)

Irina Rodnina & Alexei Ulanov (URS)
Ludmila Smirnova & Andrei Suraikin (URS)
Manuela Gross & Uwe Kagelmann (GDR)
14. Linda Connolly & Colin Taylforth (GRB)

Innsbruck 1976 (*Ice Dance included for the first time in the Winter Olympics.*)
John Curry (GRB)
Vladimir Kovalev (URS)
Toller Cranston (CAN)
10. Robin Cousins (GRB)

Dorothy Hamill (USA)
Dianne de Leeuw (NED)
Christine Errath (GDR)
15. Karena Richardson (GRB)

Rodnina & Alexander Zaitsev (URS)
Romy Kermer & Rolf Oesterreich (GDR)
Gross & Kagelmann (GDR)
11. Erika & Colin Taylforth (GRB)

Ice Dance:
Ludmila Pakhomova & Alexander Gorshkov (URS)
Irina Moiseeva & Andrei Minenkov (URS)
Colleen O'Connor & Jim Millns (USA)
7. Hilary Green & Glyn Watts (GRB)
8. Janet Thompson & Warren Maxwell (GRB)
12. Kay Barsdell & Kenneth Foster (GRB)

Lake Placid 1980
Robin Cousins (GRB)
Jan Hoffmann (GDR)
Charles Tickner (USA)
15. Christopher Howarth (GRB)

Anett Poetzsch (GDR)
Linda Fratianne (USA)
Dagmar Lurz (FRG)
12 Karena Richardson (GRB)

Rodnina & Zaitsev (URS)
Marina Cherkasova & Sergei Shakhrai (URS)
Manuela Mager & Uwe Bewersdorf (GDR)
10. Susie Garland & Robert Daw (GRB)

Ice Dance:
Natalia Linichuk & Gennadi Karponosov (URS)
Kristina Regoeczy & Andras Sallay (HUN)
Moiseeva & Minenkov (URS)
5. Jayne Torvill & Christopher Dean (GRB)
12. Karen Barber & Nicky Slater (GRB)